A Monster
HAS STOLEN
THE Sun
AND OTHER PLAYS

Karen Malpede

A MONSTER HAS STOLEN THE SUN AND OTHER PLAYS

Preface by Judith Malina

THE MARLBORO PRESS
MARLBORO, VERMONT
1987

ACKNOWLEDGMENT

The plays in this volume were first presented by New Cycle Theater, which I co-founded with Burl Hash in 1976, in Brooklyn, New York. New Cycle Theater had a patron, Ned Ryerson, whose large financial contributions provided nearly half our operating budget in the theater's first years, and whose absolute artistic support gave priceless sustenance. A Quaker, a writer and an educator, Ned Ryerson was divesting himself of his personal fortune. Many artists in this country benefited from his generosity and from his belief in the creative process. I was among the most fortunate. Indeed, it is to his unusual and farsighted vision of a way to support the arts that I owe the pleasure of those years at work in a laboratory theater, and, consequently, the final shape of these three plays. Nor would there have been a New Cycle Theater without Burl Hash, upon whose astonishing energy and plain daring all our work was built.

—K.M.

For Burl and Chris, father and son,
and for Carrie Sophia, our daughter

CONTENTS

PREFACE

"How isolated are we from one another?"

There are only a few dramatic themes, though there are myriad dramatic forms. And the question of our individuality, over and against our existence as social beings, has always been one of the basic philosophical and quotidian themes of theater, of anarchists and of women.

When Karen Malpede, one of the most consistently coherent of contemporary women playwrights, confronts this profound question, her poet's instinct and her poetical intelligence bring us these plays, which, striving so valiantly and succeeding so theatrically, present the unremitting struggle of women to change the ancient formula of Eros and Thanatos to a renewed vision of Eros and Tokos. . . . Not love and death, but love and birth. . . .

Obsessed with birth, as the male playwrights have been obsessed with death, she confronts the contradictions with a vision that undoes the old order, inverting history's mirror to reverse the traditional drama of power and death.

In each of these plays the birth is enacted over and over, recited again and again, as the central contradiction becomes clear: Why has the source of love and creation been somehow distorted into being the cause of hatred and annihilation?

Malpede shows us that the male preoccupation with conception is past history. Sexual obsession, that ever-hungry worn-down theme of sex sex sex, is only a *partial* ecstasy, in these plays becoming the background for the fruition of that act upon which the playwright focuses our often reluctant attention.

In these three plays she examines rituals from three periods of human history: the classical, the Celtic, and the modern revolutionary. And in each of these plays, the women—of Sappho's school on Lesbos, in the 6th century Celtic island kingdom, on the battlefields of the Ukraine during the civil war—the women resist: they resist the death of love, they resist the kingship, they resist the war's violence.

They are poets, they are peasants and priestesses and partisans. They are often wicked, but mostly wise. And as we read we should ask ourselves the question that the participant present at the performance must perforce ask herself: "How isolated are we from one another?" This is the woman's disquisition with which she troubles history with her disturbing light.

In *Sappho and Aphrodite*, the ritual is a rite of love, and the hymns are taken from the great Sappho's songs; the rite is the pouring of the libation, and the objective is the renewal of creativity.

In *A Monster Has Stolen the Sun*, the ritual is the struggle for power, with the sacrifice of the human/animal establishing the rulership; this ritual is overthrown by the woman who reverses the rite, and the objective is the kingdom of the happy children.

In *The End of War*, the ritual is the war itself, and the women are inside it, raped and recruited and bringing forth its children. The objective is the anarchist Utopia. But Malpede knows that there is no anarchism (liberty) without pacifism (peace). And here the means—the ritual has become war/violence—are so clearly in contradiction with the end—a peaceable world—that the child, the fruition of the commerce between vulnerability and ruthless courage, conceived on the battlefield, is born dead.

In *Sappho and Aphrodite*, the women, whose dedication is to love and to poetry, reject each other. In the first scene, Sappho rejects her lover because "the feeling . . . has died." In the second she rejects, in turn, her daughter's request to perform the central role in the ritual-play, and then, her faithful musician's. What are we to make of these rejections—our senseless suffering in the name of love?

Malpede knows well the writer's art, and unlike the romantics who pretended that suffering was the great spur to creative productivity, she shows us Sappho curtailing, then stopping altogether her song-making.

In the flower of her tragic weakness, Sappho brings us to the ritual play, a mild and beneficent pouring of libations and clasping of hands. They sing of "changing desire for death into sensations of love."

Yet finally it is in the role of the goddess of death that Sappho returns to her lover. The longing is fulfilled after all, the day of the play is over, and the world falls into place, for such a rite was possible in Sappho's school.

In *Monster* and in *Sappho*, the structure of the ritual is that of a play within a play, as in Pirandello's favored form. The play is a ritual play because the entire play fulfills the ritual in a way that the internal play-ritual fails to do because it needs renewal, is outworn, is the old king's antiquated rite, or the fading poetess's tempered religion. The play demonstrates the inadequacy of the old rites even while presenting them in the light of the awe they spread around them. . . . Even while entrancing us with the staged sacrifices of the Celts, and the majesty of the women's processionals like those fixed in marble on the sarcophagi of antiquity. The sacrifice of the goat is not a real sacrifice, and when the sweet rite of pouring libations gives way to the Great Encounter with Death in the cave, still, Death is not death, but Sappho, and the tragedies end happily.

These historical adjustments are intrinsic to an understanding of Malpede's philosophy. She shows us cruelty, all right—she isn't shy speaking out about murder—but in the ritual, she can no more imagine that her feelingful, passionate heroines could slit the trusting beast's throat than that they could slay the expendable human being on the altar. For *this* would make them more unaware than Malpede's characters can ever be.

For they are not historical re-creations. They are the highest expression of our inner beings. We are their allegories. We are the poet's struggle to renew the fount that is Sappho. We are the fierce struggle for our individuality that is the Celtic woman, Macha. We are Malpede's peacemakers.

Karen Malpede is one of the few dedicated pacifist playwrights of our time. Like many pacifists who really think through what a peaceful way of life entails, she is an anarchist, and an activist who dedicates her time, already generously given over to her family love and her wide circle of literary friends, to participation in the theoretical development and organization of peace work, and the actual practice of nonviolent resistance.

Her feminism consists in acting upon the resolve that women's capacity for tenderness shall make gentle a brutal world. Her authorship fulfills this resolve's intention.

Therefore, the ritual of *The End of War* has a particular place in these three plays. Here, the spectacle has grown all out of proportion, as it has in our daily lives. The play within the play is none other than the revolution, and the revolution has become war.

The ritual that was pure, whose goal was liberation from oppressive forces, has become a male war game. Death is really death, and the sacrifices are real men and women and children, and the ordinary lives of people are dwarfed by the great spectacle of the degeneration of the struggle for freedom into a bloodbath for power. In this maelstrom, the women, each in her own way, tries to create a liveable world. All of them are enamored of the brutish hero, all of them drawn into his war, enacting his gruesome ritual, even those who resist him, for he is "our man" and cannot be displaced until we get off the battlefield.

Karen Malpede has gathered together from times and places in our history and in our myth, the particulars of woman's profound resistance to the forces of destruction. She has put into the mouths of her wise women an uncluttered poetry that reaches back into historical cadences without losing the essence of the spoken voice, for the speaking of relationship is everything for this intrepid woman, whose hopefulness brightens our lives with exemplary action and penetrating situational studies.

Like those of the giants of dramatic writing, her works are a single oeuvre, one essential work of which each new play is a necessary next component, each one completing its predecessor. We can imagine the progression. We know for what we are longing to happen next. . . .

—JUDITH MALINA

THE END OF WAR

The End of War was first presented by New Cycle Theater on November 10, 1977. It was directed by Burl Hash, with a floor design by Michael McBride, and costumes by Sally J. Lesser and Kathleen Smith. The cast was as follows:

OLD MOTHER	Elia Braca
GALINA	Martha Elliott
ELENA KELLER	Dolores Brandon
VOLINE	Tom Gustin
NESTOR MAKHNO	David Laden
NIKOLAI	Jim Gold
THE RAPED WOMAN	Jan Cohen
UKRAINIAN PEASANTS	Jan Cohen, Riva Rosenfield
	Gary Smith, Mary Stapp
	Milton Stewart, Doyle Warren

The End of War was next produced by New Cycle Theater at The Arts at St. Ann's on May 19,1982. The musical score was by Noa Ain.

CHARACTERS

THE OLD MOTHER, GESIA
GALINA, *a newly freed serf; later, Nestor Makhno's wife*
ELENA KELLER, *a revolutionary*
VOLINE, *a poet and revolutionary*
NESTOR MAKHNO, *revolutionary leader of the anarchist movement in the Ukraine*
NIKOLAI, *Gesia's son, a peasant, imprisoned along with Nestor and Voline, demented*
PEASANT MEN *and* WOMEN, *members of Nestor Makhno's army and their women*
THE RAPED WOMAN

SETTING

The Ukraine during the Russian Revolution, 1919-1921.

In memory of Julian Beck

SCENE ONE

[*A bundle of rags in the middle of the stage: two women huddled together at the gateway of Butyrki Prison, Moscow. On the streets, the Russian Revolution is taking place, but the sleeping women know nothing of this. The MOTHER lifts her head and speaks.*]

MOTHER: Get up now, girl.
    Go your way again.
    The streets are quiet, now.
    You can walk through them.
    Take your skirts away from mine.
    Pull your legs back under you.
    Gather yourself and go.
    You have been too mixed up with me all night.
    Your head lay in the dark cradle of my arms.
    Your hair wound round my hair until sad gray
    became bright black again and black became the gray
    it's not yet been. Put on your shawl and leave me here.
    Gather yourself and go.

GALINA: I've no place to run.
    Late last night my master turned me out.
    "I can find a girl in France to light the lamps
    and pick the breakfast rose. You can go free. See
    if the peasants' laws suit your gentle beauty
    better than the harsh rule of the Tzar."

MOTHER: Can you cook well?

GALINA: Yes.

MOTHER: Do you sew?

GALINA: I do.

MOTHER: Can you spin?

GALINA: I can.

MOTHER: Can you churn butter, knead bread, make cheese at the same
time?

GALINA: And sweep, lay the fire and spin!

MOTHER: Children, do you like them?

GALINA: I could grow to care for them.

MOTHER: My son will be wanting a wife any time. Perhaps you will do for
him.

GALINA: Is he handsome and strong?

MOTHER: Broad shouldered and kind. The prison gates will open soon, you'll
see him with your own eyes.

GALINA: What was his crime?

MOTHER: Going out when he should have been home. Holding his ears
when I told him to hide.

GALINA: Have you waited a long time for him?

MOTHER: Twelve summers and all the seasons in between them, sleeping on
stones.

GALINA: How will you greet him?

MOTHER: First, I'll scold him:
Twelve years you've been gone.
Who sowed the grain?
The forest you planted can almost be cut now.
The cow has calved twelve times now.
The roof leaks when it rains.
The horse limps along on three shoes.
Then, he'll cover my mouth with his hand,
throw back his head and laugh.

GALINA: What if he never gets out?

MOTHER: I'll see him this day.

GALINA: Is his sentence up?

MOTHER: The hearts of his jailors have softened.

GALINA: How did it happen?

MOTHER: How does water change a stone?
    Last night while you lay shivering in my arms
    I dreamt a new dream the first time in twelve years.
    In my dream, the Tzar came to me,
    he took my face in his hands:
    "Mother, what has been done to make you suffer
    and grow old before your time?
    I didn't know," he said.
    "I didn't understand."
    When I woke the stones under my head
    had changed into your soft flesh.

    [ELENA KELLER *enters with a large bunch of flowers.*]

ELENA: Butyrki Prison has been taken. The gates are open.

GALINA: Your dream is true. You'll see your son alive today.

ELENA: Who are you waiting for?

GALINA: This woman's son was thrown in prison twelve years ago for no
    crime she knows about.

ELENA: A brave boy, no doubt. He's been kept where the bravest have been
    kept. Voline is here. He is the revolution's poet. Nestor Makhno's with
    him. He is the revolution's hope.

GALINA: Her son's a peasant lad. He is no braver than that.

ELENA: Nestor Makhno was a peasant, once. A slow, dull hulk drawn behind
    two oxen and a plow.

[7]

MOTHER: My lad plowed from well before the sun came up
till well after the sun fell.
But while the sun kept back the dark, light streamed
in purple shadows down across his shining back.
Then he seemed the golden lad he was;
his path shone equal to the sun's.

ELENA: Maybe he took that momentary light in
and maybe its memory changed him
until he could no longer plow in the darkness
land that was not his own.

GALINA: Was it so with your friend, Nestor Makhno?

ELENA: I was Nestor's light and he was mine. It was through an act of mine
that Nestor changed. "I never understood before that actions could
make us free," he said, as he hid me in the well behind the barn. When
he came to bring me bread the following day, his back was straight, his
eyes were clear. "I shot the soldier who came to find the police chief's
murderer," he said. "Come," he lifted me onto a horse. "The blood of
the oppressors on our hands is a more certain bond than any wedding
pledge." And so it was. I thought my death would be the consummation of my act, but found instead a keener life than I had lived.

[*Two men enter,* NESTOR MAKHNO *and* VOLINE, *half dragging, half carrying a third
man, who has been brutally deformed in prison. The three women look at them in
silence.*]

ELENA: Nestor, in honor of the life to come.
[*She presses the large bunch of brightly colored flowers into his hand. He takes them,
but cannot speak.*]

VOLINE: Elena! — meeting us with flowers at the prison gates. . . . You've
been faithful all these years, but how else would you have been . . .

ELENA: Who is that man?

VOLINE: A peasant lad, destroyed for hiding leaflets he could not read. He
was kept near us for years. The three of us tapped out our plans in code
on sewage pipes inside the prison walls. Day by day, his tapping made
less sense. Often we would hear him cry out in the night the way a
cornered fox cries at the hungry dogs, half in terror, half in joy that the

long, lonely hunt is over and the merciful surrender finally begun.

MAKHNO [*letting go of the boy, who drops to the ground*]: It's a fine joke, don't you
  think?
  Freedom. Freedom for all demented men.
  There. There's freedom. Do you want some?
  I would have died for freedom once.
  I would have hung gaily,
  or faced a firing squad with pity.
  I would have let the chains rot my head from my neck
  rather than confess. This morning
  someone I've never seen opens my cell and says
  freedom's come and I must live for her.
  What does he know of freedom who never lay
  beneath the lash and felt the cool breeze blow soft
  across his back before the lash cut deep again.
  We who have learned freedom's songs from the rattle
  of chains, what will we do with simple men's dreams?

ELENA [*stopping him*]: Nestor, please. For us, at last, the time is ripe.
  We have survived. Everywhere the people rise.
  We sowed the seeds of this great surging in the earth.
  We cannot let the crop rot in the field for lack of strength.

[*The* MOTHER *and her* SON *recognize each other. They crawl towards one another and
embrace. She rocks him and looks into his eyes. They make the happy sounds of mother
and infant. The others stand silent, watching this display.*]

GALINA: That's what we'll do with freedom.
  We'll be as trusting as that peasant mother.
  She loved her boy when he was young and strong;
  she doesn't love him less today because he's less
  than she imagined he'd become. Her dream of him
  was a cold, bloodless thing. His body's warm,
  his heart beats out a rhythm that's his own.
  When she holds him for a while she'll think he has grown
  strong again. What we know is never
  strange and what we come to love is beautiful.

[NESTOR *sees* GALINA *as if for the first time. He pulls away from* ELENA *and goes to*
GALINA *with the flowers, and presses them into her hand.*]

[9]

MAKHNO: Here, peasant girl, simple child.
　　You will have these flowers,
　　and with them, all my empty heart can offer.

[GALINA *caresses the flowers.* ELENA *and* VOLINE *are left standing alone and apart from the two couples, the* MOTHER *and her* SON, *the hero and his bride.*]

SCENE TWO

[NESTOR MAKHNO, VOLINE *and* GALINA *return to Gulai-Polye, in the Ukraine. They are met at a crossroads by people crawling towards them, crying for bread.*]

THE PEOPLE [*approaching on their knees*]: Bread!
　　Bread! Give us bread or shoot us.
　　Bread! The land is barren. It cannot feed us.
　　Our newborn drop from dry breasts.
　　The Lord's vengeance is hard upon us.
　　Bread! Give us bread or shoot us.

[*The sight of the peasants' miserable submissiveness angers* MAKHNO. *He rises to the occasion.*]

MAKHNO: Stop crawling toward me like penitents.
　　Here is one loaf. Should I divide it among you
　　or should I eat it myself in front of you?
　　Hunger is easy to share. Food belongs to the one
　　who takes it and who has teeth in his mouth to chew it.
　　Stand up. I'm not God's messenger
　　or the Tzar's tax collector.

　　I'm Nestor Makhno. Son of the people,
　　born son to a serf in Gulai-Polye.
　　I know what you know,
　　hunger, hard work, fear,
　　but I've been to the city.
　　I spent nine years locked in a dungeon.

　　Nine years below ground;
　　one endless winter.

Never one spring or one summer
to warm me or feed me.
I lived through my death
and was resurrected.
Do you know who set me free?
Starving men stormed the prison gates.
Men like you gave me sun again.
Now we'll free the land for them.
Bread can be begged from the priests by the women
but freedom and land must be taken.
Stand up. Pick up knives and axes.
Comrades, we are one another's saviors.
The earth we walk upon is ours.

THE PEOPLE [*now on their feet*]: Land! Freedom and land.
Land! Give us land or die.
Land! We'll take what we need.
Give us land or die!
Give us land or die!

[MAKHNO *leads the peasants off to take possession of the land.* VOLINE *follows.* GALINA *sits down to wait.*]

WOMAN: Where is Nestor Makhno?
Doesn't he hear his mother calling?
Where has Nestor Makhno gone?

GALINA: He's gone with the men to take land.
He'll be back when the deed is done.

WOMAN: Hasn't he heard? The landlord's sons burned his mother's house to the ground. They shot his brother through the head. His mother clawed out the eyes of the one who held her and ran screaming for Nestor into the fire. She burned like a witch. Her red, beating heart is all that is left. Do you think your charm is stronger than hers was? Do you think you're safe because he said he loved you once?

GALINA: I'll wait here for Nestor.
Who will tell him what happened if I don't wait?
Who will comfort him if I can't?

WOMAN [*laughing a wild laugh*]: Men give their faith to the strongest man.

[11]

Women give all they believe to love.
But revenge is what rules us.
Revenge is how fate plays with us.
No one is free of the wish for it,
not the ones who fight, not the ones who wait.
All know the rule of hate.

[MAKHNO *and* VOLINE *enter from the battle.* GALINA *goes to* MAKHNO. *He embraces her, but does not speak to her.* GALINA *has no chance to tell him the news.*]

MAKHNO: Voline! Come here. Bring the book you write in. Hold it open under my hand. Now, gather round me. Can you all hear me? Can you all see me? I, Nestor Makhno, swear on the pages of the book of my friend Voline never to leave Gulai-Polye until the town of my birth is free. Every man among us will strive to kill whoever oppresses us. All who seek to exploit us will die. We can trust no one who is not one of us. Not the Germans who invade us. Not the Whites who want to enslave us. Not the Bolsheviks who claim they are one with us. If anyone comes to the Ukraine to impose laws on us or to take land from us or to make us serve their cause, they must die. I, Nestor Makhno, swear with my life to bring freedom to Gulai-Polye. Who among you swears with me?

THE PEOPLE: I'm one with Makhno.
So am I.
Will freedom bring us shoes?
Of course.
And beer?
Whisky stole from the Tzar.
Then count me in.
I swear to free Gulai-Polye or die.
Me too, I want to swear.
I'm just a woman, but I'm with you.
I'll follow Makhno anywhere.
Me too.

MAKHNO: Well sworn. Let's go drink to it.

[THE PEOPLE *exit.*]

VOLINE: Wait, Nestor, you've sworn a fine oath before your soldiers and they've replied in kind. But war shortens everyone's memory. In a month or two if all who watched are dead and if you and I also die, what remains of what you've done today? You've sworn your oath, now I'll swear mine. Give me your dagger to swear on. I swear never to touch this or any other weapon . . .

MAKHNO: One battle makes a coward out of you.

VOLINE: To the contrary, one battle moves me to make a hero out of you.

MAKHNO: You think men fight for no other reason than to put words into the mouths of poets?

VOLINE: Men fight for many reasons that would all die with them if a poet did not think to leave a meaning that will live after them.

MAKHNO: What gets done remains, Voline, not what is said.

VOLINE: Nothing is done that is not first dreamed deep in the solitude where dreams begin. When your hands and feet were chained you used your aching skull to bang your love of freedom through the rat-infested wall. I heard your call and answered with my own, and another would have, if he had found the words to share the terrible longing that consumed him. Nestor, your deeds require words that reissue as their own from the hearts of other men. Let me serve you in this way. I will keep the people faithful to your cause.

MAKHNO: Give me back my knife. I release you from orders to bear arms. The man who makes myths must be free of the deeds myths are made from, just as the one who does what needs to be done must be freed from the need to remember.

[MAKHNO *cuts his arm with his knife. He offers the bloody arm to* VOLINE *to kiss.*]

MAKHNO: Let us seal our pact. One of us cannot exist alone. My deeds and your words unite now and for all time.

[NESTOR *exits.* GALINA *starts after him.*]

VOLINE: Galina, don't hurry away. The longer he waits for his soup the better it will taste to him. The more you hold yourself from him the happier he's likely to make you.

[13]

GALINA: As long as my happiness is measured by his safety, he's not ever likely to make me happy. It's not bad enough he's sworn to continue fighting, his best friend has sworn to glorify suffering.

VOLINE: You judge me too harshly.

GALINA: I don't judge you at all, but I have an oath of my own to make.

VOLINE: To whom will you swear?

GALINA: To my own ears.

VOLINE: On what . . .

GALINA: I'll swear with my feet on the earth
my head in the air
with the wood for the fire
and a bucket of water
held in my arm.

VOLINE: What will you swear?

GALINA: I swear that my words will not be separate from my deeds.

SCENE THREE

[*The camp.* VOLINE *sings to the troops.*]

VOLINE: Sometimes circumstance
makes a hero of a man
who neither wished it
nor wanted it so.

A single injustice or terror
turns farmer to warrior
while his fields cry for seeds
beneath the boots of soldiers.

Bewitched by some unknown charm

this man leaves all he loves behind:
the child his wife carries in her arms,
the new son she grows for him inside.

Who knows where his courage
comes from, how it thrives,
or why one man's brave deeds
might need a hundred lives.

MESSENGER [*hooded, in man's clothes*]: Who's in charge here?

MAN: We're all equal here.

SECOND MAN: Say what you want to say. Each one of us has ears.

MESSENGER: Keep your wits about you. Don't confuse me with what I have to say. It's bad news I bring.

MAN: If it's bad news, that's a good reason to share your burden equally.

SECOND MAN: Though the messenger comes as a stranger, misfortune is well known to us and we no longer fear her.

MESSENGER: The words I speak sound harsh to my ears, if not yours, yet I say what I saw with my own eyes. A thousand Whites took Bol'Shaya last night. They burned Bol'Shaya to the ground. They herded the men together in the square and made them watch while the women and children were raped, then thrown down the well. Each man who begged the soldiers to stop had his head hacked off.

THE PEOPLE [*keening their lament*]: Bol'Shaya is lost.
    Gulai-Polye is next.
    Where can we run to?
    Who should we hide from?
    How will we know them?
    Who can help us?
    Who can save us?

    [MAKHNO *enters.*]

MAKHNO: Who spoke the madness that led to this?
    What sorcerer took my people and with a few

idle words drained their strength and left
them weak and whining on the earth?
First, I'll undo your evil spell and give
them back their sense. Then, we'll free Bol'Shaya
and kill the men who have misused her.

MESSENGER: I didn't come to challenge you,
or to turn your friends away from you.
I came to save you.
Escape with your lives. Hide.

MAKHNO: Who are you?

MESSENGER [*turning away from him*]: Masha Kovalskaia.

MAKHNO: A woman dares give me orders.
Go sit by the fire with the others.

MESSENGER: Maybe you remember my brother, Nikolai, a fine, strong boy?
He was with you in Butyrki Prison. He's mad now. And maybe you
remember my mother Gesia? She slept twelve years on the cold prison
stones just to be near him. Each day, she begged the guards for news of
him; each day they told her he was fine and promised she'd see him if
she'd wait out the afternoon. Here, look at the heroes courage gets
you.

MOTHER [*leading her demented son*]: Come, come Nikolai.
Soon we'll be home in Bol'Shaya again.
I dreamt last night of the Tzar. He pities
his poor peasant lads. He looked hard into your
eyes. He built you a fire with his own hands.

NIKOLAI: Land. Land. Give us land or shoot us.
Land. Land. Give us land or let us die.

MAKHNO: The fight for freedom doesn't end with the wreck of one old
mother's son. Join your loss to ours.

MESSENGER [*keeps her face hidden from him*]: You didn't hear my words. I saw the
whole of Bol'Shaya destroyed. Every man who waved his scythe in the
invader's face was butchered with his own thirsty blade. They are a
hired force. A peasant's life is less to them than a stalk of wheat a

peasant gives his life to grow. We know each hill and crevice of this land. Let's hide. Let them waste their strength on a futile chase.

GALINA: Nestor, listen to this woman. Turn around and warn the rest of Gulai-Polye. We'll hide. The Whites will find an empty town.

MAKHNO: Go sit by the fire and be silent. You hear the words of one frightened girl and all you think to do is parrot her. Perhaps the women of Gulai-Polye would welcome our disgrace. Do we hide while the Whites rape our wives or do we free Bol'Shaya and avenge the dishonor already done? I'll go alone, with ten men or thirty.

MEN: I'll go with Makhno.
I will.
I'll go, too.
I'll avenge Bol'Shaya.
Comrade, take my hand. I'm one with you.

PEASANT WOMAN [to her man]: Speak up, you coward. Or do you want me raped?

MAN: All right, I'll go.

ANOTHER WOMAN [to her man]: I'd be raped before I'd have you dead.

ANOTHER MAN: What good would that do? I couldn't look at you again. I'm one with Makhno.

MEN: I am, too.
Me, too.
Count me in.

VOLINE: Then all of you, come, gather round. Galina, dry your eyes. Your love makes you greedy for his safety. But he can neither be son to a single mother nor husband to one woman. Here is a man who risks himself for many, who sets himself above a single love. Nestor Makhno, before this battle, I reclaim for you the old honored title *Batko*. You are "Father" to the thirty men who follow you to rout one thousand. Through the courage Batko asks of you, you each will rise above the limits of your isolated lives. Alone, you would live out your days unknown. Now you've found parts in a larger story. Follow Batko into battle. Your legend on earth will grow as you fight through this glorious day.

MEN [*chanting*]: Batko has our faith. Our pride.

[*The* MEN *and* WOMEN *exit.*]

MOTHER: Here Nikolai. We'll wait here for the Tzar.

GALINA: How like his old jailors
    his new followers have become. They cannot see
    their strength apart from their claim upon
    his life. Today he gives away the chance to
    live outside the cruel devotion of the crowd.

ELENA [*who is disguised as the* MESSENGER]: Yes, and all the people relinquish
    is their lives.
    What is this cause that embraces all
    yet passes by the sacrifice of each
    without a pause? What devouring beast
    moves us, naming itself justice?

GALINA: Now that I see your face,
    I know your voice.
    You're Elena Keller, the woman who met Nestor
    outside Butyrki Prison. Why didn't you let him
    see you?

ELENA: I couldn't plead with him if he saw my face.
    I couldn't let him call me coward in my own name.
    There is a bond between us that is as yet unbroken.
    Once we worked like brothers building one another's houses.
    We moved as close as horses in a single harness.
    We hid for days so near in thought we all but forgot
    the difference in our sex and yet the rush of desire
    often fused us till danger and the deed we'd done
    had both been overcome. When he turned from me to you
    that day he left behind a trust uncommon in our time.
    And, now, numb, since that moment numbed me, I cannot tell
    if I came here to warn him or to humble him. If I could
    choose I don't know if I'd choose to be his follower,
    executioner, savior, wife, or to be Nestor Makhno himself.

[18]

SCENE FOUR

[*Bol'Shaya was saved by* NESTOR's *men but then seized by the enemy again.* NESTOR's *troops have retreated to regroup. There is a momentary lull.* VOLINE, *with pencil and pad,* GALINA, *with a shirt she is embroidering,* ELENA, *silent, rest together underneath a tree.*]

VOLINE: What's the matter, Galina, has inspiration fled and left you idle, too?

GALINA: It's hard to embroider defeat. Here, on the front, I've stitched the rout by our thirty of one thousand enemy men, but the news Bol'-Shaya has fallen again leaves the sleeves and back desolate. Among the women who have done this work before me, hardly one could have been spared some dread loss in battle, yet where in their endless labor was there room for anger or for fear, for hate or for revenge, for all the feelings that lead men to war and that poets sing of? Nestor lives — my fingers should be racing with that news, but they are stiff with centuries of inexpressible grief.

VOLINE: Your simple craft delights the eyes of those who if they heard your soul's cry would turn and trample hard upon its truth.

GALINA: No one has turned on you, Voline, not yet. When you spoke to men of freedom they took up the theme and gave it richer by a hundred voices back again. When you christened Nestor *Batko*, they responded with a trust so strong it led everyone up to the point of death and some beyond.

ELENA: There's the evil lie to art, the artist's sin. You've made pain wonderful. Gained sentences from sorrow. You've turned murder into fate. Given permanence to hate.

GALINA: The poet doesn't invent these things. The people give them to him.

ELENA: A single poet, through word or action, might yet imagine what for their heroes' sakes whole peoples crowded into images of slaughter can't. What if Helen had refused to go to Troy? What if her will was such that she said "No"? What if Athena let Achilles die right at the start? Homer's epic would have been reshaped and all the men who choose to follow violent ways would have to do it without the poet's praise.

VOLINE: The poet's praise or blame are equally absurd in times like ours and if, because of some horrible curse known only to him, the poet's voice cannot be stilled, he has no choice but to give it to the common cause.

ELENA: You've let your loyalty blind you. You've forbid yourself the poet's right to be separate and apart.

VOLINE: Once I lived alone, apart from other men. There
was no fear, no grief, my heart could not contain and
tongue heave up again transformed. I thought the poetry
I wrote, by changing single consciousness, would change
social life itself. I endured the prison years knowing
this one task would save me. Though the one I loved through those
dark prison walls could speak of nothing but revenge.
Even when free. . . when his love became lost to me and we met
like two mourners and smiled the smile smiled at the grave
by slight acquaintances, I still felt the force within me through
which each grief is changed. But others stumbled underneath each
loss, many more were beaten down, until even I could not go on.
Beauty, passion, imagination became so much dust upon a monument
called human suffering. I disowned the isolated exaltation
I had known. I took up the fight that will enslave me until
the cause itself gathers up the strength to free me.

ELENA: Freedom is not a burden to be disowned, Voline. Once won it might be won again. The bravest thought becomes a shackle to the mind and must be thought beyond. The effort's all, Voline, renewing itself through rest. The effort to give shape to what we long for is the only part of life that is eternal.

VOLINE: What's done by every man becomes the only pattern that we know. The evil done is all that is passed on. Once bent into that broken mold each one repeats it by bending others to it.

ELENA: To let another suffer less than we have suffered, that supernatural act would be sufficient proof of grace to comfort us. The inequality of pain through time should be the sole inequality we know once we can trust the end of war is worth giving form to:

[MAKHNO *enters*.]

MAKHNO: My friends, talking to the traitor in our midst. The fall of Bol'Shaya saddens two of you. Does it amuse the third? Do you think it proves you right? Should we have run instead of fought?

ELENA: I think it proves the shame of war, a shame in which we each have equal share.

MAKHNO: The only shame is fear. Fear of what winning a war must mean. I liberated Bol'Shaya with thirty men. Thirty men chased away one thousand while the peasants stood and watched us free them. Bol'-Shaya was free before I left her, and would have stayed so. The trembling of the common heart betrayed her. When the enemy returned, Bol'Shaya fell to her knees. While peasants in the front and back were slaughtered, peasants in the center raised their voices to pray louder. Small animals caught in traps give out odors calling their captors closer. Freedom is dead in Bol'Shaya. Peasants whored for pity rather than defend her.

ELENA: A people afraid of their strength cannot act.

MAKHNO: Once you had the will to teach them to pick up arms and live.

ELENA: I killed a man as an example to others like him who seek their immortality in murder. I asked no one else to die for what I did.

MAKHNO: There was a peasant boy who heard you. Your deed transformed him.

ELENA: I didn't think to live beyond my act. Then the deed was done and I lived on. You want me to lie down with the act again and claim its issue as my own. But I renounce the marriage bed where once the best was wedded to the worse in me. Why is it that the worst is all you care to know of me?

MAKHNO: Value what you did however you want to. Your deed remains and will live on, though you turn traitor to the cause whose needs have proved too great for you.

ELENA: I found the lie outside my heart as well as in it. That peasant boy grew up and as he grew I watched him harden and turn cold. Though his soft curls and simple laughing ways once gave me back the will to live when I had lost it.

[ELENA *exits.* MAKHNO *waves* VOLINE *after her.*]

MAKHNO: What were you talking to her about?

GALINA: Poetry and an old war.

MAKHNO: What war? Who won and how?

GALINA: After ten years fighting for the return of Helen . . .

[*He grabs her, they begin to tumble in an embrace.*]

MAKHNO: Fair Helen, if time can be exchanged for passion
at least ten years have passed since last
I saw you sitting underneath this tree.
Yet you seem fresher than the morning air to me.

GALINA: If Helen's conquered
the war's been won.
The man who's done it
must know how it's been done.

MAKHNO: The soldier has amnesia
looking at his bride.
Who could care for war
when one can win at love?

GALINA: Dissembling is the tactic the Greeks used.
An artful maneuver, not unknown to you,
useful when the use of force won't do.
To end the war with Troy that would not end
the Greeks hid inside a wooden horse
and sent it to the city under siege.
Awe before the wooden horse caused the Trojans
to forget their own town's defense. At that
moment, Greek soldiers leapt to strike admiring
heads from Trojan shoulders.

[22]

MAKHNO: Enough . . .
>I'll borrow the ancient trick
>but use a vehicle modern people wonder at.
>I'll steal a train and fill it with our men,
>then sneak our forces into every station.
>Our daring will stir the idle peasants
>who love fine stories like the one you told
>but fear persistence in the art of war.
>In a week the Ukraine will be free;
>Voline will have a school to teach his songs in,
>you'll have your belly full of a son.
>I'll be lazy, drunk and out of work.
>Till then come be with me.
>We'll share a taste of victory.

[GALINA *and* MAKHNO *exit, arm in arm.*]

SCENE FIVE

[*The peasant men and women enter amid much excited laughter and talk. The mission has been a success. Everyone is high on the victory as they gather to name the first free commune in the free Ukraine.*]

FIRST MAN: You should have seen the station master's face when he tried to inspect our train!

SECOND MAN: He was even more surprised when Makhno's bullet hit him straight between the eyes!

THIRD MAN: Peasants came from everywhere to welcome us. They jumped aboard our train. The girls, the girls, we took them anyway we could.

FOURTH MAN: In the next town, a wealthy man was talking to some troops. We tied him up and let him watch while men he had hired to kill us dug fresh graves then leapt before our bullets into them.

FIFTH MAN: Batko asked the wealthy man if he though we were his equals now. Icily, he shook his head. So Batko hacked it off!

[23]

FIRST MAN: News of the victory train raced in front of us. Everywhere the people cheered. Virgins spread their legs. Their fathers filled us up with so much beer we could not tell if we shot friend or foe as we sped along toward home. Heroes of the free Ukraine. Feared by everyone.

[VOLINE *moves to silence the crowd, and to turn their energy around from tales of war to work of peace.*]

VOLINE: Comrades! What does it mean
  to learn how to read
  when before
  you've just known
  to make war?

  How do you still
  the desire to kill
  and end
  the compulsion to own?

  Learn skills.
  New deeds make creative wills.
  Learn to think.
  There are more than enough
  thoughts to go around.
  Knowledge increases
  once it's found.

  Learn to write.
  There's immortality in art.
  Learn to read.
  War makes heroes
  out of fearful people.
  Words make poets
  from the same material.

FIRST MAN: Voline, what do we do with the evil we've done?

VOLINE: Remember its causes; forget the old responses.

FIFTH MAN: What do we do about evil men?

VOLINE: Learn to follow yourself, not them.
  When evil can walk the Ukraine unaided

its back will be as bent as the good peasant's.

FIRST MAN: When evil has to do its own hard work . . .

FIFTH MAN: It'll die while it's young and be buried in the dirt.

SECOND MAN: When evil has to live on bread and salt . . .

THIRD MAN: Evil will be judged by its friend, guilt.

FOURTH MAN: When evil has to harvest what it sows . . .

FIFTH MAN: Hunger and thirst will be all it knows.

VOLINE: Brothers, fathers, sisters, mothers,
    all those in between,
    today we have to name the first free commune
    in the free Ukraine!
    Anyone who has a thought
    put your thought into a song like we have done
    and sing it out!
    Anyone who has an answer
    put the answer in a rhyme.
    The finest song
    will contain the finest name.
    However far the spirit moves you
    that's how wonderful the sound.

FIRST MAN: Our commune must have the name of a great revolutionary leader.

FIFTH MAN: Batko Makhno.

VOLINE: Sing about it.

FIRST MAN: I don't think I can.

FIFTH MAN: We'll try it together . . .
    Batko Makhno . . .
    Batko Makhno . . .
    Batko Makhno . . .

Batko Makhno . . .
led us into battle!

FIRST MAN: And we followed him . . .

FIFTH MAN: Through dirt and death . . .

FIRST MAN: And back again . . .

FIFTH MAN: To our free commune!

VOLINE: Good! Go on.

FIFTH MAN: Deniken came with the Whites.

FIRST MAN: Trotsky came with the Reds.

FIFTH MAN: Batko snuck behind them
    and hacked off all their heads.

FIRST MAN: The Whites bled red
    and the Reds bled red
    and I looked at the ground and thought
    the blood of men is all the same
    but how different are their hearts.

FIFTH MAN: We wanted some land where we could farm
    and a town where we could build
    but the Whites bled red
    and the Reds bled red
    and kept us from this work.

VOLINE: Good! Very good! But should we pick the first name we've heard?

GALINA: I'll sing a song that explains how Batko Makhno already has a
    bearer of his name.

VOLINE: Go ahead, Galina.

GALINA: In the middle of the battle
    on a bloody afternoon, life came
    inside my empty belly

[26]

and whispered to me, "Life remains."

With murder all around me
and fear cowering in my breath,
life squirmed its way inside me
to hide a little while from death.

I, the frightened woman,
frightened for the man I love,
let him go to free the city
while life fluttered in me like a dove.

If he had died that day in battle
I would have mourned for near a year,
but one day the long lament would leave me
for life itself must limit tears.

So all you men who fight for freedom,
all you men both brave and true,
leave your seed inside a woman.
Then death can't have the best of you.

VOLINE: It seems Nestor Makhno's going to have a son. Should he have a commune to carry on his name as well?

ELENA: There's a woman, not of our country, who herself died bravely in service to ideals not unlike ours. Hear my song. Perhaps you'll name the commune after her.

[Sings]

Rosa Luxemburg is dead.
Rosa Luxemburg is dead.
She was killed last night.
She was killed last night.
Who killed her?
Army officers beat her.
Drunken men killed her.
Why did she have to die?
Why did she have to die?

She spoke against war; she said: "Unrelenting revolutionary activity coupled with boundless humanity — that alone is the real life-giving force of socialism. A world must be overturned, but every tear that has flowed and might have been wiped away is an indictment; and a man hurrying to perform a great deed who steps on even a worm out of unfeeling carelessness commits a crime."

She who had such passion in her heart
aroused such hate.
Why is that?
Rosa Luxemburg is dead.
Rosa Luxemburg is dead.
She was killed last night.
She was killed last night.
They took her shoe when they threw her in the river.
What did they do with her shoe?
What did they do with her shoe?
They drank champagne from it.
They drank champagne from it.

MAKHNO: Let Rosa Luxemburg be the name of our first free commune. She suffered enough for this gift, leaving a song on a brave sister's lips, while Nestor Makhno's army will leave a thousand sons behind, each one a tiller of this fertile ground.

VOLINE: Is Rosa Luxemburg the name we choose?

ALL: Yes!

MAKHNO: Well done, Elena. I learned something.

ELENA: It's been long since you looked at me long enough to learn from me.

MAKHNO: And long since you left me. Your eyes have been harsher to look upon than the barrel of Deniken's gun. The words you spoke were rougher than the Bolsheviks' fire.

ELENA: The soldier left his lover standing at the prison gates, he was the one who did not look back.

MAKHNO: He was consumed by other things. His fever dream of freedom turned him into a leader of men and caught him up in other men's needs. Now the victory is won and he must go back to where the dream began, to sunset on the steppes and our great plans. He needs to hear his lost girl's voice rising amid the evening songs of the birds and the reckless answers of the frogs. He wants to delight in harmony in which he's had no part, to be comforted by shadows and the golden light and led beyond the soldier's hardened thoughts ... Elena, we've waited for so long. I have grown strong enough to bend to your great will. I want to share this peace with you.

[ELENA *and* MAKHNO *exit, arm in arm.*]

MOTHER: Galina, come sit by the fire with me.
You're ripe as a purple plum tree
but your man can't see.
He's off with the one with the silver tongue,
whose belly's as hard as a log,
who fears what she does,
fear shows in her eyes.
He'll come back to you.
The woman who gets them
when they're wild like that
is the woman who waits.
She'll run as soon as he's touched her.
He'll be back when she's gone,
bringing flowers from the field
where they've lain.

GALINA: What gives him the right to walk through the world like this, churning the earth under his feet, seeding the barren plot, leaving me wild and lush ...

MOTHER [*singing*]: I had a lover who went to war
singing, "If I ever get back
bring me a pear."
I had another who caught a fever
singing, "Give me an apple,
I'll tell you a fable."

His fable was short;
his fable was simple:
peasant, fighter, factory worker
share one power all together.

There's no escape from rape, young girl.
There's no escape from rape.

I gave him an apple,
he held it above me,
he was a believer in patriarchy.
The one I gave the pear to left me,
all in the name of anarchy.
There's no escape from rape, dumb girl.
There's no escape from rape.

SCENE SIX

[Once MAKHNO's troops had rid the Ukraine of the Whites and the people had begun to establish independent communes, the Bolsheviks decided to take over the Ukraine and they turned on the Ukrainian anarchists once again. Trotsky's troops marched into the territory and, then, the Whites also returned. MAKHNO's followers were beaten; the anarchist movement was destroyed.]

VOLINE: Peace didn't last,
 how could it?
 Gulai-Polye was invaded;
 Reds from the north swept through her
 followed by Whites from the south.
 Liberators and oppressors each
 raised swords over us.
 Threatened by peace
 they ended the moment of peace we began.
 Elena left to bring help.
 Makhno's army hid on the steppes.
 The women and children who lived
 abandoned the town of their birth
 and ran after the men.
 Every time the broken army turned
 around to hide from the enemy guns
 they found the image of their
 own defeat beind them.
 Wounded women and battered children
 lived in the dust
 raised by the feet of the soldiers.
 What was left of the army could not flee

what was left of the town.
They were of one flesh, after all.

[*Dressed in a priest's vestment he has found on the battlefield, leaning on his mother, the demented* NIKOLAI *chants.*]

NIKOLAI: In the last days perilous times shall come. For men shall be lovers of their own selves, covetous, boasters, proud, blasphemers, disobedient to parents, unthankful, unholy. Without natural affection, truce breakers, false accusers, fierce, despisers of those that are good. Traitors, heady, high-minded, lovers of pleasures more than lovers of God. Having godliness but denying the power of God: from such turn away, for of this sort are they that creep into houses and lead captive women laden with sins, led away with divers lusts . . .

RAPED WOMAN: Bless me, father, for I have sinned.

NIKOLAI: The Lord will bless you, for He is good.

RAPED WOMAN: Oh, my God, I am heartfully sorry for having offended Thee. I detest all my sins. I detest in myself the causes of them and all the pride that led me to them.

NIKOLAI: The Lord will bless you, for He is good.
The Lord will grant absolution unto you.
What have you done, daughter, what have you done?

RAPED WOMAN: I have witnessed many things. Many foul, unclean deeds have I seen. I could not stop them, but neither could I turn my eyes away from them. Bless me, father, for I have sinned.

NIKOLAI: The Lord will bless you, for He is good.
The Lord will grant absolution unto you.
What have you seen, daughter, what have you seen?

RAPED WOMAN: I saw an old woman, yellow with age. Her cracked breasts hung on her yellow flesh. I saw her taken by soldiers. I saw them, one after the other, plunge into her. "Mother, mother," they cried. Each one, in turn, buried his face in her chest and begged for the love of her who had already died. And though they cried, they did not stop abusing her. Neither did they notice she was still. Only I saw all this. I could not stop them, but neither could I turn my eyes away from them.

Bless me, father, for I have sinned.

NIKOLAI: The Lord will bless you, for He is good.
 What have you seen, daughter, what have you seen?

RAPED WOMAN: My child. My child. A girl of seven, sweet smelling and
 young, her golden curls like angel's breath blessed her sweet face. She
 was too small to receive them. One took a dagger from under his belt.
 He sliced open the sweet pink flesh between her legs. "Baby, baby," he
 cried. But she, terrified, could not cry, neither could she run. Her
 strong young legs lay useless under her, split apart by a knife. "Flesh of
 my flesh," I cried. "My child, my child," I cried. I could not stop him, but
 neither could I turn my eyes away from him. Bless me, father, for I
 have sinned.

NIKOLAI: The Lord will bless you, for He is good.
 The Lord will grant absolution unto you.
 What have you seen, daughter, what have you seen?

RAPED WOMAN: The same soldier entered me. My dead daughter's first lover
 turned from her to me and he plunged himself into me. He roared and
 he groaned while her young body grew cold on the floor. Still I
 breathed and still I saw. Bless me father, for I have sinned.

NIKOLAI: The Lord will bless you, for He is good.
 Give of yourself to the Lord and you will know
 goodness the rest of your days.

 [NIKOLAI *falls on her, as if to rape her in his turn. The* MOTHER *watches.* MAKHNO
 enters with GALINA. *He pulls* NIKOLAI *off the* WOMAN. GALINA *is now quite*
 pregnant. She moves slowly.]

MAKHNO: Dog. Enough. I've seen enough without having to see this. You
 won't breed a race of lunatics while I have breath. Get to the front with
 what's left of my men. And you, get back with the rest of your sex.

 [GALINA *begins to go with the* MOTHER *and the* RAPED WOMAN; MAKHNO *pulls her*
 back.]

MAKHNO: They go on their own. You stay away from them.

GALINA: Who else will comfort them when their hero turns his head away?

MAKHNO: They're past comfort now.

GALINA: Am I any less unclean than the women who follow behind us? Because I went to your bed willingly did you use me any more lovingly than your enemies used them? Their sin is branded on them openly, but mine is burned as deep inside. I know what I am. You pretend I'm clean because your own needs have to stay pure in your own eyes. But I've watched while without wishing to you recoil from my smell. I've seen how you despise the same flesh you enter through. Even now my ripeness angers you, though its fruit is yours.

MAKHNO: Galina, for kindness's sake add one bitter truth to the bitter truth you spoke. Defeat has wronged me far more than ever I wronged a woman. I loved you as well as I was able. I loved Gulai-Polye and lost her, too.

GALINA: You did not love her as she was. You sought her only as she might become. The simple moment never gave you pause and now the simple life is lost.

MAKHNO: No loss can take the memory of love away, though love be all in the past and the rest of our lives spent desolate, no loss can take the memory of love away. In silence, at strange times, the memory of love will come, the wretched longing rise. Then I know how it was with us. How, while war raged all around, I found a place to rest within your arms.

GALINA: My swollen frame is proof that love once had returns. The day we made this child was pure. Nothing had hurt us so badly then that we could not love again. And, now, the pure begotten child spins. Each quickening the promise of a love renewed.

MAKHNO: Galina, wife, whether I've earned it or not, woman inside whose flesh a part of me revives, can you also save Gulai-Polye? It's a desperate thing I ask, but I have no choice. We are a conquered people if we do not stage this fight. There is one chance we might reclaim our land. I've sent Elena through the enemy lines to find some men under Trotsky's command who have grown loyal to our cause. They will sell us guns and, for a price, will fight along with us. Take this map to her. If she receives it in good time, all is not lost. We'll meet in three days, advancing from two sides and begin our attack in the place I've circled here. We'll stage a battle which, if desperation gives us strength, might bring us the peace to raise our child . . . Galina, wear this while you go. It was my mother's cross. May it keep you safe until you are back within my sight.

GALINA: Many times I've tried to leave you to the other woman you have loved, but always as I crept around the corner I always thought I heard you whisper "Stay." So I kept my body rooted to a spot where you could find it, and I willed my heart be still. Now you send me off to bring Elena back and with her a victory she's bargained for. I will do as you ask, wearing this cross you've hung around my neck.

[GALINA *leaves.* VOLINE *enters.*]

VOLINE: You should have sent me in her place. The route is overrun with Trotsky's men.

MAKHNO: A pregnant woman can travel unsuspected. Your face is on the posters next to mine. "Wanted. Two anarchist criminals. Nestor Makhno and Voline." [*He laughs.*] Together we've caused quite a row. Besides, Voline, how could I have sent you off before a fight? In better times, we used to walk the fields all night, stopping for a drink at every soldiers' camp. When we could hold no more we fell asleep beneath a tree or in a ditch and dreamt of victory or of some woman's lingering touch. Come, Voline, it is a night like that.

VOLINE: Yes, we'll be comrades one more time.

SCENE SEVEN

[*Before the battle. Two groups of sleeping bodies.* VOLINE *and* NESTOR MAKHNO *intertwined. The* MOTHER *and her son,* NIKOLAI, *intertwined.*]

VOLINE: The soldier lies sleeping in my arms. He has spent the whole night sleeping sound. Though I thought to wake him when the first dread images appeared, some long forgotten self took hold of me. I could not move. I sat watching the past do a slow dance of the dead on the rim of my own dim consciousness. I saw each corpse of those who died for this great cause. Each one turned his hollow face and beckoned with his hand. But when I strained to see where they had gone, the heart beat of the soldier in my arms made my sight grow dim.

The soldier sleeps on undisturbed. Have you forgotten all those prison nights we waited to be shot when I held you while you cried and you held me until the sun rose on brave composure and strength? Or in the silence of your solitary sleep have you, also, been visited by ghosts? Will you wake and look me in the eyes? Silent, do you know the waste of those brave men who, killing, died?

MOTHER [*halfway awake, still twined in the limbs of her son*]: I dreamt I gave birth
    to the worst sin on earth
    and it hid itself under my skirts
    where it lived until it grew big.

    I, among all of my sex,
    was chosen because of my age,
    my brittle flesh and sour milk,
    to give birth to the worst sin on earth.

    Only I would continue to live
    while the worst sin on earth dug
    its teeth into me and ate itself free.
    Only I would not die of this birth.

MAKHNO: Voline, Voline, move, Voline, move off me. I'm full of the most wonderful dream. But it's no wonder I dreamt of prison, you're pressing in on me closer than the prison bars. I dreamt of a magic ring. It was a talisman, fashioned by the great goddess of the social revolution, the radiance of all-conquering love in her eyes. She stood at my bedside, a gentle smile on her face. Her arm extended above me, half in blessing, half pointing toward the dark wall — there, in a crevice something luminous glowed. It was a heart-shaped ring. Impulsively, I reached out and plucked the ring from its dark corner. I put it on my finger and suddenly its rays burst into a fire that spread and instantly melted the iron and steel and dissolved the prison walls, disclosing green fields and woods and men and women playfully at work in the sunshine of freedom. Then something dispelled the vision. Voline, your weight took the dream away.

[*The* MOTHER *crawls toward* MAKHNO. *As she goes, her son wakes and cries out for her.*]

NIKOLAI: Maaa . . .

MOTHER [*her bad dream now dispelled*]:
    Blessed Mary, Mother of God, we are saved,
    here is a wonderful son, strong and brave.

NIKOLAI [*cries*]: Maaa . . .

[VOLINE *goes to him.*]

MOTHER [*attaching herself to* MAKHNO]: I was too long at the cross.
    I was too long mourning for your loss.

MAKHNO: Evil-smelling foul old hag.
    Hardly the goddess I need.
    Life gives off bitter laughter
    after such a dream.
    Where is the joy I knew in my sleep?
    All my friends and followers reduced
    to this stale mass of useless flesh,
    while, in my heart, the dream still rages.
    There's a plot for you, my friend.
    Hide these ugly facts in some spell-
    binding song and use it to stir
    up the will to win inside my men.

[MAKHNO *exits. The* MOTHER *follows him.*]

NIKOLAI [*lets out a final cry of loss*]: Maaa . . .

VOLINE: Turn your dull head toward the uncomprehending sun.
    Drink up the warmth that men can't give to other men.
    Remember, if you can, the month or two we spent when
    Nestor and you and I could reach each other once or twice
    a day through those dark prison walls. We were happy,
    then, stroking one another's matted hair, touching cracked
    lips between the damp, chipped prison bars.
    We three were prisoners of the state.
    I did not dare to think men's own pure hearts
    would dare exact a punishment as great.
    Here we are in one another's arms.
    Once again, he's fled. Tonight, we may all be dead.

Nothing is left except this passionate connection
which endures despite violent recognition
of need that cannot be filled.

SCENE EIGHT

[*Having successfully brought the guns to the reinforcements of* MAKHNO's *army,*
ELENA *and* GALINA, *very pregnant, joined by the old* MOTHER, *wait near a lake while
the battle is fought.*]

GALINA: The moon is a victim of heavy, tumultuous clouds. They open and
close jaw-like around her. What is temporary and low eats up the high
permanent light. The moon is full in the power of her captors now.
Her light is fully out. Will the elemental fight above spare us from the
terrible fight below? Now, the belly-full clouds turn radiant. A glow
from the world's lost soul, gentle and wonderful, lights the sky from
within. The grass on the steppes, the lake water turn luminous. We
will be spared nothing at all by the moon's forced absence.

ELENA: The first dull rumble of the guns rolls through the earth toward us
and thunders back again toward where the battle has begun. Nestor's
deep in danger now. Voline behind him. And all the other lesser men
we once smiled upon are far past any wish of ours to save them. Each
one has given up his heart to war.

MOTHER: Women, what have you done,
giving guns to men you love,
sending your men to war?
Women, what have you done
trading your power for the power of a gun?
You have come so far from when
you lived at peace, apart from men.

Women, what have you done,
trading your power for the power of a gun?
One by one you let men lead you
away from the houses of your mothers
and your mothers blessed you.

[37]

One by one, you learned to love them
beyond all others
and your daughters forgave you.
One by one, you bore men sons,
adored them and sent them to fight.
Love and hate formed a knot
deep in the pattern you wove;
helpless before it you let
men rip it apart with their swords.
Now you've begun seasons of war
without end.
Women, what have you done
trading your power for the power of a gun?

ELENA: The catalog of all your sins assails me
equally as my sins assail you.
It is a book of pages without end,
what women have done and will do again.
You watched while the ruined flesh you
gave birth to once poured his lust
into woman after war-stained woman.
"He has a right to them," you said,
"the defiled have a right to the defiled."
Wasted with weak, hurt with hated,
bent with stunted mate,
the worst of life survives.
This is the union you've allowed.

GALINA [to ELENA]: You ran by my side, your hand in mine,
through enemy lines, past newly-burned barns,
over fields that were plowed
but not planted. When I stumbled and fell
you steadied me. When you lost the way I found it.
We did not speak, nor could we,
not from fear of being caught
but because cold hatred for the other body that we
touched had silent hold on all our thought.
You had lain wrapped around the man I love
and with your arms and legs and wild insatiable heart
had used me up to give him strength.

ELENA: You spread yourself, defenseless, on the hill

while our proud eagle picked away at you.
Every time he drew blood, you dug your nails
deeper into the new wound and screamed. Whenever
someone asked you to be strong, you cowered behind
the mask of weakness you'd put on and cried out against
the same abuse you craved. You eat your own flesh.
The destruction you commit is criminal, yet it has been
sanctioned for all time. The sacrifice of self
is the single wrong we might grow beyond.

MOTHER: My lost daughters, speak no more.
    It is the cry, unadorned and pure,
    the cry of the wounded heart I hear.
    In a wild flight let the cry soar,
    turn, be transformed and changed until
    forgiveness comes to pulse in the same spot
    where once the wound was all that could be felt.
    Death and dying dance together,
    Dance until they disappear.
    This is a night for our rejoicing,
    This is a night for our rebirth.

    Spin three times around.
    See your face in the lake each time.
    The first time round say who you are.
    The second time round say what you wish.
    The third time round take what you need.
    This is a night to heal wounds.
    For one moment all is different,
    all is changed,
    all is as it could have been
    had women not suffered other's pain.

GALINA: I see a jealous face in the lake.
    Jealousy is not my face.
    Who can be jealous who can give birth?
    Jealousy's a spell that I've been cast in,
    undo the curse, undo the curse.

ELENA: My face is the face of one expression,
    my face is the face of absolute diligence,
    perfect correctness. Make my face multiple

[39]

and various.

MOTHER: For one moment all is different
    all is changed
    all is as it could have been
    had women not suffered other's pain.
    Spin three times around.
    The second time round say what you wish,
    see your face in the moon this time.
    This is a night to heal wounds.

GALINA: I sought a kindness I had never felt
    and sought to wrench that unfelt kindness
    from the numb place inside myself and so fill
    up the world with it that it would fill my heart.
    I thought the loneliness would end.
    I did not know that out of longing only longing comes.
    Now, while I'm full of the unexpected, I can feel,
    as if for the first time, the stone I have made
    of the kindness I longed for.

ELENA: I have wished that the world be changed
    and have given my strength for that wish
    ever since I awoke from the empty privilege
    of my noble birth full of the cry of the dispossessed.
    But only now have I grown innocent enough to wish
    the changes on this changing earth might each begin
    with us tonight, with what we know and what we've dreamed,
    and what on this moon-blessed battlefield we might become.

MOTHER: Death and dying dance together.
    Dance until they disappear.
    This is a night for our rejoicing.
    This is a night for our rebirth.
    Spin three times around.
    The first time round say who you are.
    See your face in the lake this time.
    The second time round say what you wish.
    See your face in the moon.
    The third time round take what you need.
    See your face in whichever face you choose.
    This is a night to heal wounds.

GALINA: Look how the water reclaims a face I have feared
    by washing away each hard, impenetrable glance.
    Now I see the gentleness beneath your strength
    and sense your own tenderness and warmth.

ELENA: Not the water, but your keen, caring sight has cracked
    apart the stony sculpture of my face. I always thought
    the wild energy I felt must be tamed by someone
    larger than myself or it would set me far
    apart, exiled, alone, marked for my whole life,
    but now I know I needed warmth and someone
    gently brave enough to let me live out my
    highest self. I could not have seen myself until
    I saw my dreams reflected in the deep pools of your
    eyes. All my sorrows would not have made me wise.

[*The two women embrace.*]

SCENE NINE

[VOLINE *bursts in on the women. The battle has been lost.*]

VOLINE: Nestor's wounded in the thigh and bleeding hard. Our men were
fighting well until they saw their hero hit. Then they put down their
guns and ran to him. They formed a wall of flesh around the hero they
have loved. Many were shot and are left bleeding on the field we have
fled. Many died protecting him. We have to smuggle Nestor out of the
Ukraine.

[*A peasant enters.*]

FIRST MAN: We'll use the fastest horse. Let Trotsky's men kill each and every
one of us. As long as Batko lives the dream won't die.

[*Other peasants enter carrying* MAKHNO *on a litter.*]

FIRST MAN: I'll get a cart to put Batko in.

SECOND MAN: I'll get some straw to lay him on.

THIRD MAN: I'll get a horse to pull the cart.

[*Cheers and activity.* GALINA *has been listening all the while as she kneels next to* NESTOR. ELENA *stands, watching the two of them.* VOLINE *begins to undress* NIKOLAI, *who has entered with the peasants.*]

VOLINE [*handing* NIKOLAI'*s robe to* GALINA]: Galina, hand Nestor's jacket here. Our men will take him to the border in the wagon. You'll have to find a way to smuggle him across. There are friendly guards at Vasil'Kov. I'll go another way with the Mother's son wearing Nestor's coat. We'll let Trotsky's troops see us go and let them come chasing after us.

ELENA [*taking* VOLINE *by the shoulders*]: I'll go to Trotsky. I'll bargain with him for a fair peace for Nestor's men. I'll remind him of our exile days when we three sat together in cafes, before the chance for power made strangers of us all.

VOLINE [*hugging* ELENA]: Galina, take Nestor's jacket off.

GALINA [*she stands*]: I can't, Voline.

[VOLINE *bends, removes* NESTOR'*s jacket and smooths* NESTOR'*s brow.*]

ELENA [*embracing* GALINA]: Go with him, now, for me. He may yet live to see his child.

GALINA: I cannot go, Elena. Nestor has to go alone. I cannot follow any more. If everything that every peasant's fought for depends upon the single life of a single man, it doesn't matter if it's Nestor, Trotsky or some other crueller than either of them. Someone whose power has yet to be imagined will surely come. He's being conjured at this moment in the minds of millions who think their chance for life depends on sacrifice to someone else's high ideals.

ELENA: Go with him, Galina. Save yourself and the child.

[VOLINE *kisses* NESTOR.]

VOLINE: Farewell, my friend. Galina, come, take his hand. He's feverish and weak.

[42]

[VOLINE *dresses* NIKOLAI *in* NESTOR's *coat.*]

Come, lad. You are the real hero of this tale. If I live, I'll write a song for you. If we die together on this day we leave a humming in the air, an unsung song for unborn men to sing.

[*They go. The* MOTHER *cries out, but does not follow them. She is going to go with* NESTOR.]

FIRST MAN: Lift Batko up.

SECOND MAN: Gently, gently, now. Woman, come. He needs a wife to wipe his brow.

GALINA [*does not move*]: Bear your hero off.

ELENA: Go. Galina, go. Take your chance for happiness.

GALINA [*places her hand on her big belly*]: My chance for happiness is here, within, and cannot be claimed by watching peasants die to smuggle Nestor out of the Ukraine. Stay with me. The child will soon be born.

ELENA: I have to go to Trotsky first. If I live, I will come back to rock your child.

GALINA: You can't bargain with an angry man. He'll torture you, or worse.

ELENA: Perhaps, but there is no one else who can negotiate with him. Someone has to work a peace for the Ukraine.

GALINA: Elena, give up the fight. It will not end until we give it up. Think of your own life and of the single truth your life might tell.

ELENA: My life . . .
So much was asked of me always.
So much demanded in answer to the terrible times
in which I found myself.
I though the burden would be lighter
if I shouldered only common hopes and common dreams.
My life ended when I was a girl.
It was fixed when the shot I fired fell
between the brass buttons on the police chief's chest.

Part of me withered and died then. Part of me hardened.
And part of me thrilled to that violence.

[*She lets go of* GALINA's *hand.*]

GALINA: Elena, when we stood together all last night you named a fuller
self.

ELENA: Yes, but it must wait.

[ELENA *kisses her and leaves.* VOLINE *enters carrying the body of the son,* NIKOLAI.]

VOLINE: He's dead. They shot him in the back ten times before we'd gone
ten yards. And left me unharmed. [*He laughs, a bitter laugh.*] Now I can
write the song I promised him.

GALINA: Leave him here with me. I will lay him out.

VOLINE: You stayed. You loosened Nestor's hold on you the minute that he
needed you.

GALINA: The minute that I saw him plain.

VOLINE: Elena's gone to Trotsky's camp?

GALINA: Yes. And seeks from that hard man the same compassion that she
has.

VOLINE: I'll go and lend my voice to hers. Once we knew him well. He was
not bad. He wanted what we wanted, then.

GALINA: Yes, before he tasted blood.

[VOLINE *leaves.*]

The Mother's son, "gone in the head," she often said. "Not what he
was." But how unjustly dead. Left without a mother to mourn you.
She's run off with the soldiers. An old woman who can barely walk,
chasing after the mongrel pack. How hard the need for heroes dies. Is
it any wonder Nestor lives beyond you? A thousand and more lives
create him: mothers and their sons, men who might have loved,
children, horses, dogs, women like me who give off a spicy smell

whenever he passes, women like her, brilliant and brave, all the riches of the natural world in service to a will that's not our own. The earth that might have been green darkening and dying, the final burnt offering. Through it all the wish for heroes lives and we endure beside it: the image of the unborn child, the corpse and the lone woman wait.

[*Night falls.*]

SCENE TEN

[VOLINE *enters carrying* ELENA, *unconscious, in his arms. The sun rises.*]

VOLINE: Galina, Nestor is safe because of this bruised shape I carry in my arms. She stood firm in front of Trotsky's rage, refusing to tell where Nestor went. For it, she's been beaten and abused. She cannot walk, nor talk, nor understand. Mend her if you can.

[GALINA *goes to* ELENA. *She settles her heavy frame down next to her.*]

GALINA [*crooning comforting sounds to* ELENA]: Elena, look. Open up your eyes. Here we are. The two of us again. Hush, now. Hush. Let me wipe your brow.

[GALINA *makes little comforting noises. She lays her cheek to* ELENA's *cheek. She touches her flesh to* ELENA's *flesh. She blows breath on* ELENA's *face. She hums to her. She works slowly and carefully to restore life.*]

VOLINE [*holding* NIKOLAI's *dead body in his arms*]: Here is the son. The same boy I loved I have let die so that a cause worth more than his embittered soul might survive. I thought to make a hero of him in the end. I promised I would sing for him. But when he died, I felt my own breath stopped. Now, the tuneless corpse lies singing in my arms. "Care for unborn things," he sings. The words hum in my blood.

[ELENA *stirs in* GALINA's *arms;* GALINA *supports her as she speaks.* ELENA *gathers strength as she tells her tale.*]

ELENA: In my prison cell where spiders, lice and fleas were all the bounty of

[45]

this bounteous world thought fit to keep a woman company who would not obey or in the cold room where they beat me when I would not answer them, I learned no one can destroy the part of me that can respond to kindness only. Alone in that dark prison room, I found myself untouchable and strong. Alone, I found the strength to say, my torturers have no power over me. You can kill me, but my will goes free. You can cover me with anger and force me to receive your rage, but there is a part of me you cannot touch and that one part survives. Angered by the impudence in my eyes, they raped me with the muzzles of their guns. "Talk," they whispered in my ear. "Tell us where he went." I shook my head. They pinched my breasts, slapped my face, raped me again. The world will perish in such hands as theirs. The earth will punish her unfaithful sons. Man makes his own destiny but he makes it only once. Unless the whole pattern is reversed and in each head a wakening occurs and in each heart a way to love what we most fear is found. I've grown old before my time. I'll die too soon. But there aren't many who have known a strength like mine or felt the sacred energy I've felt or the delight of making the hard choices for the first time.

GALINA: Elena, the time has come.
I must give birth.
I must deliver myself.
Voline, come, hold me up.
Help me squat above the ground.
Elena, breathe with me. Hold out
your arms. Help me help the child out.

[VOLINE *places himself behind* GALINA *and holds her up. They begin to move in the rhythm of birth.* ELENA *comes to her and begins to breathe with her, rubbing her belly. The image is of the three of them,* VOLINE, ELENA *and* GALINA, *as near-equal participants in the birth-effort. As the contractions quicken,* ELENA *reaches beneath* GALINA's *skirts to receive the child. As* GALINA *makes the final push, we hear the birthcry.* ELENA *holds the infant in her arms, then puts it on* GALINA's *breast.* GALINA *fusses with the baby a minute, then looks up.*]

GALINA: She's dead. She died. She did not dare open her eyes.

I will lay the body of my infant daughter out
next to the body of the full-grown
defiled and defiling old Mother's son.
In quiet death the two of them will find

[46]

the union violent life forbade them.
In years the spirits that could
have been theirs will come.
If we survive and if the wish for life
inside us does not die
children will be born to us again.
A daughter and a son will come,
brother and sister, woman and man,
a race born free of sacrifice,
gentle, unafraid and strong.

SAPPHO AND APHRODITE

Sappho and Aphrodite was first presented by New Cycle Theater with Virginia Giordano at the Arts at St. Ann's and the Wonderhorse Theater in October, 1984. It was directed by Lois Weaver, with music composed by Roberta Kosse, a setting designed by Bernette Rudolph, costumes by Sally J. Lesser and Kiki Smith, and lighting by Joni Wong. The cast was as follows:

SAPPHO	Beverly Wideman
ATTHIS	Kate Stafford
ANACTORIA	Catherine Coray
CLEIS	Dorothy Cantwell
TIMAS	Edwina Lee Tyler

On December 15, 1984, the play opened at the Perry Street Theater, presented by Virginia Giordano, and with the original cast.

NOTE ON THE POEMS

I have used Mary Barnard's version of Sappho (*Sappho: A New Translation*, Berkeley, University of California Press, 1958) because I found it to be the most modern and the most accessible to the ear. Occasionally, I have altered a word or two within a poem (personal pronouns for the most part) to make it fit more nearly the action of the play. In the text, lines from Sappho are followed by an identifying number enclosed in parentheses, corresponding to the number of the poem in the Barnard volume.

CHARACTERS

SAPPHO, *in her forties, mature, beautiful, at the height of her creative powers; but also beginning to feel the first and fearsome effects of aging.*

ATTHIS, *twenty-five to thirty-five, a poet whose talents are just now reaching full flower; Sappho's lover and intimate of several years.*

ANACTORIA, *twenty to twenty-five, a wealthy young woman from Sardis, a newcomer to Sappho's school.*

CLEIS, *thirteen, Sappho's daughter.*

TIMAS, *twenty-five to thirty-five, Sappho's musician; she is unable to speak. She plays lyre and drums and can make vocal sounds.*

The cast is multiracial. On stage there are five different skin colors: a rich palette, a world-community of women.

SETTING

The lyric poet Sappho ran a school for women on the isle of Lesbos. Here, women were taught the arts of poetry, music, dance, physical fitness. Here, too, they engaged in rituals in honor of the goddess Aphrodite, goddess of love and death, goddess of the creative life in women.

Many wealthy young women were sent to study with Sappho prior to marriage. Women came to Sappho's school to acquire a sensual, creative sense of their womanhood that would be strong enough to last them through years of secluded wedlock.

But there were also certainly other women living with Sappho, less well to do women like Atthis and Timas whose talents and plights had appealed-to her and to whom she offered a home to live and work in.

And there were other schools like Sappho's on Lesbos where women came to inspire each other and to fulfill themselves as artists.

In memory of Barbara Deming

ACT I

[SAPPHO's *school on the afternoon of the annual ritual to Aphrodite, goddess of love, but, previous to her Olympian designation, goddess of the creative life that is in women, goddess of life and of death. It is to these earlier, more inclusive states that* SAPPHO *and her students wish to return the goddess.*]

[*In their rooms in* SAPPHO's *school, her students make ready for the evening ritual.* CLEIS, SAPPHO's *teenage daughter, tries on endless combinations of clothing;* ATTHIS, SAPPHO's *lover and intimate of several years, writes and is occasionally taken by bursts of unspecified, nervous energy, focused in* SAPPHO's *direction.* TIMAS, SAPPHO's *drummer, readies her instrument and watches.* SAPPHO *sits on her bed and writes, occasionally she gets up and exercises.*]

[*From the distance, we begin to hear a new voice, that of* ANACTORIA, *singing a Sardinian song as she walks toward the gates of the school. We lose the voice momentarily, then it begins again.* TIMAS, *in answer, starts a rhythm on her drum. And the life of the school quickens. The women begin to sing fragments of what becomes the opening round. Sometimes they sing the entire poem, sometimes only a phrase. At first, silence returns between the snatches of song, and sometimes* ANACTORIA's *voice is heard, getting closer. When* ANACTORIA *arrives, she sings her entire song and the round begins as each woman adds her voice. During the singing and to the rhythm of the drum* ANACTORIA *dances her sensuous dance of greeting.*]

ANACTORIA: Standing by my bed

In gold sandals
Dawn that very
moment awoke me.[3]

SAPPHO: I asked myself

What, Sappho, can
you give one who
has everything,
like Aphrodite? [4]

ATTHIS: Although they are

Only breath, words
which I command
are immortal. [9]

CLEIS: That afternoon

Girls ripe to marry
wove the flower-
heads into necklaces.[10]

[*When the round ends,* ANACTORIA *continues to dance, and* TIMAS *plays for her on the drum.* CLEIS *begins to imitate* ANACTORIA'*s dance, while* ATTHIS *and* SAPPHO *stand apart, equally absorbed in the sight. Then* SAPPHO *begins to sing:*]

SAPPHO: And their feet move

Rhythmically, as tender
feet of Cretan girls
danced once around an

altar of love, crushing
a circle in the soft
smooth flowering grass. [23]

[*The dance assumes the rhythm of the song and both end simultaneously.*]

SAPPHO: Timas, your drum is the happiest welcome
we have. Happiness is the best of the gifts
you could bring tonight to the glade.

[TIMAS *plays a few happy beats on her drum.* ATTHIS *approaches* TIMAS *and places the headdress of snakes and the robe which belong to Aphrodite on her head and shoulders.*]

ATTHIS: I crown you goddess of life,
death, birth; the madness of love;
fall fruits; decay; the frenzied
creative self; and whatever else
is deserving of praise!

ANACTORIA: Hear!
Hear!

CLEIS [*gaily, to* TIMAS]: You will be Aphrodite tonight in the mime!

[TIMAS *plays a happy response, but* SAPPHO *reaches for the crown.*]

SAPPHO: That role is mine alone to decide.

CLEIS: But we promised her!

[TIMAS *plays an angry beat.*]

ANACTORIA: Does she never speak?

CLEIS: Cannot. Her tongue was cut out
    by soldiers who ravaged her village.
    My mother bought her half-starved
    in the market and taught her to talk
    on the skin of a drum. She sat
    silent for weeks and then she began to
    bang on the skin. She broke three
    drums to bits before she made up the
    wildest song we had ever heard and we
    sat from sunset to dawn weeping and
    wailing with her as she played.

[*The sound erupts from* CLEIS, ATTHIS, SAPPHO, *and* TIMAS. *It is an ancient cry, expressing both joy and grief; praise and terror.*]

Eleleu, Iou, Iou!
Eleleu, Iou, Iou!

[ANACTORIA *shudders at the sound and at the story.*]

ATTHIS: "Don't pity me," she says.
    She plays what she feels; since
    each sound is true, each is beautiful.

SAPPHO: Now, while the sun peaks, we must rest,
    for this night will bring us no sleep.
    Timas, gather the wreaths and the fruits;
    float them in water in shade. Cleis, show
    Anactoria to her room. Welcome, Ana, to us.
    You have come at the height of our year

[55]

when we inquire most deeply within and ask
for the grace to become whatever desire
dictates. Go, now, and rest; I will
call you back before the ritual starts;
I would tell you the ways of this
worship we make to ourselves. In all
Greece you will not have seen nor
heard of its like. Only here do we seek
that earlier state where no seam exists
between desire and deed.

[SAPPHO *takes* ANACTORIA's *hand. She kisses* CLEIS *lightly.* CLEIS, ANACTORIA *and* TIMAS *exit.*]

ATTHIS: I will stay. I do not feel like being alone.

SAPPHO: Come, then, and sit.

[ATTHIS *sits on* SAPPHO's *bed.* SAPPHO *approaches and gently strokes her hair.*]

SAPPHO: Do you wish silence or talk?

ATTHIS: Tell me what you are thinking while you stand idly stroking my hair.

SAPPHO [*bending and kissing her lightly on the head*]: I am thinking of you as you were the day I first saw you on the street, a long-limbed child singing and dancing behind her mother's full skirts. I stopped to purchase some parsley and thyme she carried from market to market in woven baskets strapped to her head and her back. I saw her silence your mouth as I stopped, and watched you stick out your tongue, at which one of us I still to this day am not sure, but I felt you mocking my wealth. I loved you, Atthis, when you were a graceless child and you paid no heed to my love. "Send her to me," I said, pressing gold coins into her hand. "Send her to me when the milk you fed her on first turns to blood and stains her thighs. Send her ripened and sad in the month of her first grief for what cannot live. I will teach her to sing love songs then."

ATTHIS: I did not understand a word that had passed but I saw the gold change hands and felt I had been sold like one of her bundles of herbs or sold as she sold herself in the late afternoons to the first hungering man. Yet when the time came, it was I who remembered your words and I who made ready to leave while she turned her head and cursed the quickness of years. "I will not have you go without something to bind up your hair," she said and pulled out a dark purple ribbon she had hidden between her two breasts. For the last time, she wiped the dirt from my face with her spit. "Go," she said, "go and make something out of yourself." Then she looked down at her toes, hard and cracked, the color of stone piled on the earth. Her mind has fled, I thought, back to the time she carried me miles strapped to her back with her herbs and she first heard my nonsense songs in her ears. I cried out, and saw her body grow stiff. I left without looking back and walked till I came to your house. "Come, lovely child," you said, as you fed me on milk and on figs. "You will make your home here with us. Young girls with large appetites stir up my songs of love."

SAPPHO: Did I say that? How blatant I was in my youth. Yet it took time to touch.

ATTHIS: You were as shy as I was.
Except when you lectured us.
Then, you terrified me.

[ATTHIS *leaps up. She puts her hands on* SAPPHO's *shoulders and speaks forcefully into her face; it is an exaggeration of how she remembers* SAPPHO *to have been in those days.*]

ATTHIS: "Only if we women regain our strength, might a balance be reached between the other and the self. Only if we grow less afraid can we keep hatred from the world. It's up to the women poets to sing. Up to us to recover the time when women risked everything for knowledge of self, when daughters were loved above all else, when we formed our bonds from a sacred trust. This is the cause you must take up."

[ATTHIS *lets go of* SAPPHO's *shoulders. She laughs.*]

You've mellowed over the years.

SAPPHO: I have. But the old ways worked. You, an illiterate gypsy-like girl, began to write two weeks after you'd come to my house. Overnight you became [*here she mocks* ATTHIS, *as* ATTHIS *was*] "the greatest poet who ever lived, better than Sappho, but misunderstood." Or a "failure who never again would write a word," storming around breaking things, sobbing for hours in my arms.

ATTHIS: I must have driven you mad.

SAPPHO: With your talent, your tempers and fears, you held me entranced. I
am a slave to that moment of youth when for the first time one's
power is sensed. The world seems changeable then. And you were a
monumental piece of work. A genius risen stark from an impoverished
class.

ATTHIS: Timas, too, also because of you.

SAPPHO: Yes.

ATTHIS: And the young ones are still flocking here.

SAPPHO: Most of them leave in a year.

ATTHIS: All are changed. And some show a spark that might burn. The new
girl you welcomed just now. There's something special to her.

SAPPHO: Yes, she reminds me of you as you were.

ATTHIS: Yes. She will follow wherever you lead.

SAPPHO: I am too old to fire her. I have lost the spark.

ATTHIS: Not in my eyes.

SAPPHO: The times have closed to my dreams.
    Greece forgets women's mysteries stand
    at its base. Zeus is set up over us.
    My lyrics are thought titilating, small, private, obscene
    and are grandly praised by voyeurs who name me the eighth
    wonder of the world! Nature's own freak, a woman who feels
    and dares speak. Scarcely a person outside this school
    will admit an ancient power sings through my verse.

ATTHIS: You talk like this when you are tired. Tonight, through the song and
the dance your strength will return.

SAPPHO: I need to be stirred again, by someone proud and unformed like you were.

ATTHIS: Why do you speak this way?

SAPPHO: Why speak at all? Except to give form to what feelings have bid.

ATTHIS: Last night when I came to your bed, you pretended to be asleep.
The night before, you kept Cleis tucked in your arms. I did not weep,
or cry out, or demand, but, Sappho, I am afraid.

SAPPHO: Don't be afraid. You are grown and I must let you go.

ATTHIS: I am grown and I choose to remain. Before the ritual begins, take
me into your arms.

SAPPHO: Before the ritual starts, we must practise honesty with ourselves.
You are grown and will find a new love. I must go back to the source
of my dream.

ATTHIS: You are cruel.

[SAPPHO *kisses her head.*]

SAPPHO: Something is cruel, not us.
Something, not us, yet its cruelty works in our hearts.

ATTHIS: It was you who taught me how to be kind.
Can you not be kind yourself?

SAPPHO: Perhaps, in the end, kindness is not
the best of our virtues. Perhaps
kindness is taught to silence the truth
of the heart which is seldom as kind as we wish it.

ATTHIS: Whatever is wrong, we can work to mend it.

SAPPHO: Nothing is wrong, only time. Time and my need
to defy it by being always at its beginning.

ATTHIS: Let's go back to the start of our love.
I can act simple and unschooled again.

SAPPHO: When I first kissed you, I told you this day
　　would come, as it has come, and I asked if you
　　wanted my love, though it would last but an instant.
　　Do you remember your answer?

ATTHIS: I silenced your lips with my tongue.
　　But how could I have known then
　　the end of our golden hour would ever come,
　　though you told me over and over. And how,
　　had it ended bitter and hard a thousand times,
　　could I, barely more than a child, have resisted.
　　Nor would I resist even now if you were to lay
　　your lips hot with warning upon mine.

SAPPHO: But now you must let my words in
　　though my lips resist you.

ATTHIS: You will not kiss me?

SAPPHO: Cannot. Cannot kiss you as I kissed you once.

ATTHIS: Three nights ago,
　　I came running to show you two lines
　　which had perfectly caught the start of a thought
　　that seemed crucial to me. I asked for a kiss
　　so I might finish the verse. You gave me one
　　gladly it seemed. In response, my words leapt
　　from my heart. What has happened since that
　　moonless night?

SAPPHO: The song I released in you left me silent.
　　I sat for an hour alone
　　watching the sky
　　pale into dawn.
　　When I rose I was changed.
　　I no longer felt an answering call in my heart.

ATTHIS: How can that be?
　　How can someone who held
　　my wet flesh in her hands
　　turn cold?

SAPPHO: It has happened before.
    Feeling between two lovers has died.

ATTHIS: Yes, you have sung
    of such foul things
    many times. Sung of foul
    longing and pain. Do you cast me away
    for the sake of a new image of grief?

SAPPHO: Do you cling because you wish me to drown
    in your child-like faith in my love?

ATTHIS: You are cruel to tell me today
    when my heart ought to be light,
    for my song was chosen, even over
    yours, to be sung tonight
    in the glade where we sing
    Aphrodite's praise.

    Are you jealous, Sappho?
    Jealous of my success?
    Are you jealous because
    I have put into verse
    things that you teach
    but do not feel in yourself?

SAPPHO: No. I am proud.

    In skill I think
    you need never
    bow to anyone.

    Not one who may
    see the sunlight
    in time to come. [51]

ATTHIS: The lyrics I wrote were for us.
    Remember the day we dove from the cliff
    and lost in the vulva-like folds of the sea,
    we laughed and felt safe. Later, we lay on the
    shore while the wind rose and the rising tide
    covered the rocks. "How close to death love is,"
    I suddenly thought as you opened me with your tongue.

I grew wild and cried, "I will leap to my death from
these rocks." But you held me close while I struggled
and wept and I fell asleep on your breast. Tonight's
song was to make up for that day my fear marred.

SAPPHO: As it does, for you have made an exquisite thing from your fear.

ATTHIS: But after it's acted and sung you won't call me home to your bed?

SAPPHO: After it's done I will want to know
    something else. I will want to know
    what would happen if souls could touch
    as completely as flesh. What would happen,
    Atthis, right now, if you could inhabit my
    heart and I yours?

ATTHIS: You would feel my longing and pain.

SAPPHO: Yes. And you would know
    how the limits
    age puts on dreams
    turn me desperate.
    How the lustre of youth
    abandons my flesh
    till I am left
    facing death.
    But such rare empathy
    has not been Aphrodite's
    gift to us so we have come
    to the end of our love.

ATTHIS [she begins to circle SAPPHO, *speaking in a frenzied, staccato tone*]:
    I am named for a boy
    who died young
    because a woman he scorned
    followed him
    until she infused
    a great cold breath
    in his veins.
    I am named Atthis because
    my poor mother thought
    a hard-hearted death

to be a far better fate
than the slow pain of one
who is scorned.

But it's you who should bear my name.
The pain you have caused
will turn to ice in your veins.
Both of us cannot live past what you've done.

[*From off-stage, as if in anticipation of the ritual, we hear the mourning-celebratory cry:*]

Eleleu, Iou, Iou!
Eleleu, Iou, Iou!

SAPPHO [*taking a shimmering shawl off her chair*]:
    I have kept this for you to wear
    on the eve that your words are sung
    in worship of what through love
    and love's death we become.

[SAPPHO *hands the shawl to* ATTHIS *who drops it upon the ground.*]

ATTHIS: It is not mine
    if it lacks your arms
    putting it on,
    pitiless love.

[*As* ATTHIS *goes,* SAPPHO's *adolescent daughter* CLEIS *comes running in, trailing a mess of half-woven yarn. Behind her, concerned, is* TIMAS. CLEIS *throws herself at her mother's knees.* ATTHIS *watches for a moment the girl who has taken up the place she has just left, then she turns and goes.* TIMAS *settles herself close to* SAPPHO *and* CLEIS.]

CLEIS: It's no use

    Mother dear, I
    can't finish my
    weaving
        You may
    blame Aphrodite

    soft as she is

she has almost
killed me with
love for that boy.[12]

[SAPPHO *comforts her daughter, comforting herself as well with her mothering motions. She pulls her daughter to her and sings her the same song she used to sing when* CLEIS *was a baby in her arms.*]

SAPPHO: Hush darling

I have a small
daughter called
Cleis, who is

like a golden
flower
              I wouldn't
take all Croesus'
kingdom with love
thrown in, for her.[17]

CLEIS: Why, when I love him so,
         does he scorn me?
         I brought him a handful
         of white and red anemones.
         He took them, laughing,
         then turned and ran off
         with Gryinno, that big-hipped girl.

SAPPHO [*gathering up the shawl* ATTHIS *has left behind; her tone is light and playful*]:
         My darling, what have mothers
         said since time began to their
         tender girl-children . . . you are too
         good for him! Never mind,
         if he took your flowers, he has
         taken part of your heart, and your
         goodness will work its way into him.

[*She hugs* CLEIS.]

Anyway, think, if he had turned and pulled you
into his arms, you would have been so scared
you might have kicked him or bit him.

[64]

Better he has taken what you handed him
willingly and gone than stolen a bud
that will ripen itself in good time.

CLEIS: Still, it seems I shall die
    from love of him. Feel here, my
    heart, pounding as if it will break.

[TIMAS *plays her drum, melodramatically.*]

Meanwhile, I am pursued wherever I go
by that crooked-nosed son of your friend
Andromeda, who seems to grow fonder
of me with each scornful abuse I sling
at him. "Cabbage-head," "olive-eye," "bird-
beaked squatting creature." Because I am your
daughter he fancies I speak only pure-toned
love images.

SAPPHO: If you truly spoke with my voice
    your words would have even more sting
    for all those who hunt you too soon.

CLEIS [*delightedly, as she makes this up*]:
    "Web-footed, donkey-assed
    nose-dripping platypus,
    why have you cast your pale
    leprous glance in my direction?
    Do you wish conversation?
    Your green eyes shed mucousy tears
    at the melodic sound of my words;
    my heart shudders and stops; you
    reach out a misshapen claw. I draw
    back. The snake that hangs limp
    in your lap suddenly hisses
    and rises up. As I run I can hear
    you bray satisfaction."

[*The two laugh and* TIMAS *plays a trill on her lyre.*]

SAPPHO: Cleis, your tongue is a murder instrument.
    The crass poet Archilochus so satirized a girl

who had scorned him, she and her family, in shame,
hanged themselves. And your verse, my child, is far
stronger than his.

CLEIS: But harmless, for no man would admit that.

SAPPHO: Until they can, you should keep your best self
safe from these boys. They judge our beauty as
harshly as we do theirs and delight in our softness
as much as we delight in their supple limbs. But they
remain deaf to our words, as if Zeus himself, in fear
for the power he wields, forbade them to learn a tongue
graceful and fluid. So, darling child, we will gather
tonight to worship our fair Aphrodite from whom our
best creativity comes. It seems to me, after the
song you have sung, you would do well to cleanse your
ears on Atthis's verse.

CLEIS: Mother, who is to play Aphrodite tonight? Timas would like to, I
know, but if she can't, let it be me.

SAPPHO: You are too young.

CLEIS: I am a year past menses. I have seen the mime many times. I
understand all it means.

SAPPHO [laughing]: I have no doubt that you do.

CLEIS: Then let me be the goddess tonight.

SAPPHO: You are not ready yet to dance the mad
possessed dance on the mountain tops . . .

CLEIS: I am.

SAPPHO: Not ready yet to give up a self
not yet known.

CLEIS: I am not afraid of going down into the cave.

SAPPHO: Wait awhile, child, I am well-trained to see when the time for that
passage has come. It is not a moment I would keep you from.

CLEIS: Then, at least, let me stay here and help you dress and watch you
    anoint whomever you choose.

SAPPHO: I would rather you went to help Atthis,
    and let her help you, for she loves you
    as tenderly as if you were her daughter.

CLEIS: Before I am banished,
    tell me, as you used to do,
    what I should wear.

    [CLEIS *makes ready to hear one of her favorite songs;* TIMAS *begins to play.*]

SAPPHO: Don't ask me what to wear

    I have no embroidered
    headband from Sardis to
    give you, Cleis, such as
    I wore
            and my mother
    always said that in her
    day a purple ribbon
    looped in the hair was thought
    to be high style indeed
    but we were dark:
            a girl
    whose hair is yellower than
    torchlight should wear no
    headdress but fresh flowers. [83]

    [CLEIS *kisses her.*]

SAPPHO: Now, love child, run off to Atthis and, for me, be especially kind
    to her.

    [CLEIS *exits. Silence.* SAPPHO *turns to* TIMAS.]

SAPPHO: Timas, you who keep all my secrets safe
    in the silence that shelters your own,
    forgive me my frailty one more time.
    I cannot make you goddess tonight.

    With his venom

Irresistible
and bittersweet

that loosener
of limbs, Love

reptile-like
strikes me down 53

I must give the snake-crown
to the innocent girl who
with her gay guileless charm
has swallowed my life in her own.

[TIMAS *responds on her drum, with increasing anger.*]

Don't chide me, now, Timas, please.
You can be Aphrodite next year.
But now bring Ana to me.

[TIMAS *is still angry.*]

SAPPHO: Timas, I can't help my choice.
A song has begun in my flesh and it will
sing itself.

[TIMAS *exits.* SAPPHO *begins to sing while she waits for her chosen lover to come.*]

If you will come

I shall put out
new pillows for
you to rest on, 45

I shall unwind
your braid, comb
out your hair.
If you will come
I will rub
your neck and arms
with warm oil,
take off your
sandals, caress
your cool ankles.

I will lift up
your gown,
if you will let me,
and ask if my hands
might be led
to the gate of your
heart and if they
might spread wide
the portal that
guards unguarded
delight.

[ANACTORIA's *voice is heard outside.*]

ANACTORIA: Oh, no, what have I done. I can't get my hand out.

[*A moment later she is half falling into* SAPPHO's *room. Her hand is caught inside a decorated jar she has brought as a gift.*]

Oh, Sappho, look! I was so nervous being called to your room that without thinking what I was doing I put my hand inside this jar I've carried all the way from Sardis. Now I'm stuck; I can't get my hand out; it's started to sweat; I'm trapped in this vessel I meant you to store oil in.

[*At this moment,* ANACTORIA's *hand slips free of the jar which shatters on the floor.*]

Oh, now how did that happen?
I'm free but the jar is ruined.

[*She kneels and begins to try to piece it back together.*]

That will never do.
That's Demeter seated
with Dionysus's head upon her.
And Hermes, Zeus's messenger,
stands at her side where
Persephone ought to be standing.
How like the world we live in now,
and I can't set it right again.
I can't find the goddess's head.
It must have shattered past recog-

[69]

nition. What a fine mess I've made
and to think I was sent here to learn
social graces. Sappho, how will you
ever teach such a bear? How do I dare
bumble my way into your room?

SAPPHO [*laughing*]: Hush, sweet one, hush,
  sit here, listen to what
  I will teach you:

[*She sings.*]

  Awed by her splendor

  Stars near the lovely
  moon cover their own
  bright faces
        when she
  is roundest and lights
  earth with her silver 24

  So it is
  with a woman possessed
  by her power. Not even
  the brightest star
  outshines her.

[ANACTORIA *leaps up and spins around with delight; she kisses* SAPPHO *lightly on the cheek.*]

ANACTORIA: Sappho, what a beautiful song.
  You are so beautiful
  and I am so dumb. I swear
  I can't make up a word.
  A phrase would be sheer impossibility.
  As for dancing, well, my left foot
  doesn't speak to my right.
  And, Sappho, I am not pretty!

SAPPHO: Beautiful, simply.

ANACTORIA: Do you think so?

SAPPHO: You, my heart, are the new hope
    I have longed for. You are strength and pride
    seeking direction. The thing itself, essence.
    If I have asked the goddess for a love whose needs
    would be met by my needs, and I have asked it,
    she has answered me with your presence. "Here, Sappho,"
    she whispered, "is one who will bloom as you teach her."
    Grateful, I answered: "I will choose her to wear
    the snake-crown; dancing your dance, entering into
    your unknown space she will learn how to praise you."

ANACTORIA: Sappho, stop. Atthis chose Timas this afternoon.

SAPPHO: She transgressed the limits I've set. The choice of the goddess
is mine.

ANACTORIA: It's not fair to the others who had hoped you would choose
them that I, a newcomer, am so quickly chosen.

SAPPHO: Chance sent you to me and I have chosen
    to please her. Two roles remain,
    mother and maid, who lift you, their soul,
    from the belly-like cavern.
    Chance will pick them.

ANACTORIA: Sappho, you be the goddess tonight. Let me attend you. You
are the one with frenzy and calm in her heart. I am nothing.

SAPPHO: You are the woman untouched whose touch rouses creation.
Come, heart, I will dress you.

[*She releases* ANACTORIA's *tunic;* ANACTORIA *stands in her shift.*]

ANACTORIA: Sappho, stop. I am frightened.

SAPPHO: You need only give yourself over
    to life that is in you.
    You need only let
    yourself rise when we call you.
    All else will be done
    by our voices
    rising together

[71]

and the sound of your step
on the earth, thundering power.

[*She slips a gold and black ritual garment over* ANACTORIA's *head. It falls formally to the ground. She begins to look statuesque.*]

ANACTORIA: I am not worthy of this.
Not capable yet. I have not
wrapped a lover between my legs,
nor let a child escape me. I have not
raged at the loss of youth, or of hope
for what youth should have brought me.
I have not heard my singing unanswered,
have not become bitter with longing. I
have not fought bitterness off, alone
and angry, until I grew soft enough
to let chance embrace me. I am not
the goddess you make me.

[SAPPHO *brings the snake crown to* ANACTORIA *and places it on her head.*]

SAPPHO: You are desire, desire unripe,
unripened but not unheeded.
You are what makes woman great
so we have named you goddess.

[*Now the music begins to be heard, faintly at first, then growing stronger and clearer throughout the scene. The music is timbrel and flute. The timbrel giving the beat as if of many women's feet dancing, the flute song wild, plaintive, ecstatic. It doubles back on itself from grief to joy and includes the motif "Eleleu, Iou, Iou."*]

[SAPPHO *gives* ANACTORIA *a staff like those the Maenads carry on the mountain.*]

ANACTORIA: I am not endless love, not forgiveness.
I am not one who holds the beast-like child
to the breast, who ripens and thrills
to the hungry pull of those lips.
I fear dark. I fear death.
I am not the cycle itself.

[SAPPHO *places the fawn skin in* ANACTORIA's *hand.* ANACTORIA *begins to sway with it dangling from one hand, her staff held horizontally in the other.*]

[72]

SAPPHO: You are the sorrow that smites
  and the joy that wipes sorrow out.
  You are the salt sweet underground milk
  rushing toward light, bursting the mouth
  of the earth. You are the force that binds
  wound to wound, beast to breast, life
  to death in one rhythm. Fear is the
  huntress of those who fear you.
  Fearless is she who loves you.

[ANACTORIA *sways to the rhythms of the timbrels, the music of the flutes. She is the possessed Maenad loose on the mountain, losing her fear of frenzy inside the frenzy itself.*]

[*The music and dancing peak. There is a flash of light.* ANACTORIA *is caught in a freeze at the height of her frenzy. Sudden darkness. The sound of bull-roarers.* ANACTORIA *has dropped out of sight. As the light returns we hear the lament of the women, "Iou, Iou," and we hear their chant, as if from far off.*]

CHANTING WOMEN: We have followed her step,
  her sound, her dance,
  have followed her wild
  release until
  she fell and was
  swallowed up by the earth.

  Iou, Iou!

  We have come to her grove,
  to her glade,
  to her belly-like place
  in the earth,
  bearing gifts from the grain,
  the bee, and the breast,
  bearing honey, milk and the seed.

  Eleleu, Eleleu!

  Now we choose two by chance
  who will be for us
  Mother and Maid.
  Two will approach the cave
  where womb-like, death-
  like she roots, and lay

[73]

there the fruits of the
earth, calling her up.

Eleleu Iou, Eleleu Iou!

[*As the sound of the paean is made,* ATTHIS *and* SAPPHO *approach the center from opposite sides of the space. They have been chosen by lot to assume these roles and did not know the other was also chosen.* ATTHIS *carries a stalk of golden grain in one hand and bowl of honey in the other;* SAPPHO, *a stalk of grain and jar of milk.*]

ATTHIS [*as she lays her stalk on the ground*]: None have I longed for
    more than her
    whose path I have followed
    here . . .

SAPPHO [*as she lays down her stalk*]: . . . to the center
    where all is brought
    up from the dark unknown.

ATTHIS: None have I longed for
    more than her
    whose lips I have
    longed to touch.

[ATTHIS *takes honey from the bowl on her fingers and lets it dribble down her lips; she does the same to* SAPPHO, *trembling.*]

SAPPHO: No one has desired
    her more than I
    who drinks
    of her own sweet milk.

[SAPPHO *takes a drink of milk from the jar, and offers a drink to* ATTHIS. *The following is stated; it breaks the pattern of the song.*]

ATTHIS *and* SAPPHO [*together or alternating lines*]: We are conscious of death,
    all-knowing of that unknown.
    We fear and we yearn for that end.

[SAPPHO *kneels on one side of the omphalos.*]

ATTHIS: I have wanted to curl

between your flesh,
have wanted to sleep
in your arms.

[ATTHIS *kneels beside the omphalos.*]

SAPPHO: Yet, living, I have
rejected death
and she is reborn
as love.

[ATTHIS *reaches down and grasps Aphrodite's hand.*]

ATTHIS: She is born from that dark
into us,
her soul which is love
and her flesh.

[SAPPHO *reaches down into the omphalos and grasps Aphrodite's other hand.*]

SAPPHO: Flesh of her soul
we touch
and are born into self
by this love.

[*The sound of rejoicing, flute-song. "Eleleu, Eleleu" is heard as Aphrodite rises in the classic pose.*]

ANACTORIA [*sings solo and then the verse is repeated by ensemble*]:
And I rise from the earth
or am washed ashore by the sea.
Salt is my smell, honey my taste.
Milk, which is life, I have brought.
I have changed desire for death
into sensations of love.

[*The goddess has risen. The ritual moment is over.* ATTHIS *and* SAPPHO *remain, each holding one of* ANACTORIA's *hands. More from* SAPPHO's *response than from* ANACTORIA, *it dawns on* ATTHIS *that this woman is to be* SAPPHO's *new lover, and the whole horrible irony of the ritual and her part in it flashes before her. At this moment,* CLEIS *approaches* SAPPHO, *tugging at her.*]

[75]

CLEIS: Mother, he has asked me to come,
    tonight when the ritual ended.
    He would wait, he said, at the edge
    of our circle.

SAPPHO [*to* ANACTORIA]: Come, I will take you back to my room,
    take off your dress and your crown.

ATTHIS: She is still in her trance,
    still possessed.

SAPPHO [*to* ATTHIS]: Your song is a success.

ATTHIS: Yes. Your breast rises and falls.
    Your eyes shine and I,
    the creator of this,
    go home alone.

SAPPHO: You are free to choose
    someone new.

ATTHIS: What is she but the actor
    who lives through my breath?
    What is she but my essence
    singing itself?

SAPPHO: Your anger must answer you.
    I cannot.

[ATTHIS *releases* ANACTORIA'*s hand; she squats down beside her.*]

CLEIS: Mother, will you listen to me.
    He has asked me to come.

SAPPHO: Who, Cleis, who?

CLEIS: Adonis, himself, my heart.
    He waits for me where the waterfall
    wets the dark earth near the apple trees.

SAPPHO: What are you talking about?

CLEIS: Mother, please, I've no time to chat.

SAPPHO: The boy you gave flowers to,
    who scorned you this afternoon?
    Or is it the boy you scorned?
    Who wants you to come when you
    are full of our song?

[SAPPHO *lets go of* ANACTORIA's *hand. Continues to address* CLEIS.]

    You will come home with me tonight.

CLEIS: I will not. I should have just left. I shouldn't have told you a thing.

SAPPHO: If he loves you, whoever he is, he'll understand.

CLEIS: What do you know!
    You who refuse to lie with a man.

SAPPHO: I conceived a child in love with a man.
    A child whose love I will keep until
    she knows why she gives it up.

CLEIS: Let me go. He was right. He warned me not to tell.

SAPPHO: Come with me, Cleis, we'll sing
    one another to sleep.
    Tomorrow you'll see him again
    in the hot noonday sun.
    Decide then if you want his love.

CLEIS: The minute I've closed my eyes, you'll call to your bed whomever you
    wish and you'll make love through the night. And the minute you do,
    I'll run off.

SAPPHO: Come home with me now,
    you determined child.
    We can't argue here in the glade.

[*She turns to* ANACTORIA.]

    Ana, dear, follow us home.

[SAPPHO *and* CLEIS *exit.* ANACTORIA *blinks out of her trance.*]

ANACTORIA: Oh, my head aches from this crown.
　　I'm dripping with sweat.

[*She smells her underarms.*]

I smell like sour milk!
My feet are cut.

[*She inspects one foot while leaning clumsily on* ATTHIS*'s shoulder, then she sits down
hard.*]

I'm so tired.

[*She laughs, gaily.*]

A fine goddess of death and desire I make!
Do you suppose Aphrodite herself felt like this
walking to shore over those rocks, climbing up
out of the earth, and no one cared how she felt?
Poor girl, Aphrodite.

[*She laughs again.*]

Atthis, help me take off this crown of snakes.
Too bad they're stuffed, I'm so starved I could
eat them up. If I ate snakes, that is, which
I don't.

[ATTHIS *laughs with her and looks at her. Then she rises, offering* ANACTORIA *her
hand to pull her up.*]

ATTHIS: Come,
　　I have figs and nuts
　　and a cold clay jar full of milk.
　　I will lay them out
　　next to your thigh.
　　We will eat
　　and be full
　　when we rise.

[ATTHIS *and* ANACTORIA *exit.*]

ACT II

[SAPPHO *is alone in the glade where the ritual took place. A small brazier burns incense outside the cave where the goddess Aphrodite is worshipped.* SAPPHO *paces. Dawn.*]

SAPPHO: Tonight I've watched

The moon and then
the Pleiades
go down.

The night is now
half-gone; youth
goes; I am
in bed alone. 64

[*She glances at the paper on which the verse is written.*]

What pale fragments
you wring from me now, Cyprian,
I who once decked your altar out
with tales of clustering girls, ripe as moons.

[SAPPHO *tears the paper.*]

My mind is swollen with words,
the path from my room to this spot
littered with words I've thrown out
and the truth is untold.

[SAPPHO *feeds the pieces of paper into the brazier; they burn.*]

Greedily, as if I sang with full throat,
you lick up my slight thoughts.
And the longing on which they barely touch,
can you soothe that with your tongue-like flame?

[79]

[*From off-stage we hear* ANACTORIA's *voice, singing.*]

ANACTORIA: "And I rise from the earth
    or am washed ashore by the sea.
    Salt is my smell; honey my taste.
    Milk which is life I have brought.
    I have changed desire for death. . ."

I wonder if I dare alter that line? Well, there's no one to hear.

[*Sings.*]

Milk which is life I have brought

and I have been blessed
with all the fruits of the earth.

[ANACTORIA *enters; she bears an overflowing cornucopia, her gift to the goddess who has blessed her so richly with love.*]

Sappho, I didn't see you!

SAPPHO: You have come singing Atthis's song. Yet you altered a line.

ANACTORIA: It was too eery sad for my mood.

SAPPHO: "I have changed desire for death into sensations of love." It is the death wish in Atthis I sought to change but could not. Never mind. You did well to come.

ANACTORIA: I woke at dawn. An expectant sense woke me up. What can I bring to her who has everything, I wondered out loud, and Atthis said, "Bring her the fruits of our love." You see how literal-minded I am.

SAPPHO: Yes. I hunger and thirst. You come bearing fruits.

ANACTORIA: I brought them to lay at the door of the cave for I have been richly blessed.

SAPPHO: By Atthis, and by myself.

ANACTORIA: Sappho, you blessed me the moment I heard your voice. Your lyrics have taught me so much.

SAPPHO: Were you called by my song?
    A longing half-formed
    like the half-form of our love?
    Can a need that gives birth
    to pale and wrong images
    make you believe in its truth?

ANACTORIA: I was singing as I came. I didn't hear your song.

SAPPHO: Can you think how bitter it is
    when hundreds of women once danced
    to your words not to be able to speak
    in a voice a single woman can hear?

ANACTORIA: I was just passing by. I'm wrestling with Atthis as soon as the
sun warms the ground.

SAPPHO: See how my words fail me.
    I have not been able to sing
    since I put the goddess's crown
    on your head. My words have
    lacked power since then.

ANACTORIA: I know . . . it's whispered about. But, Sappho, it happens to
everyone, doesn't it? Atthis says you have been silent before.

SAPPHO: Does she? What else does she say?

ANACTORIA: She says silence serves its purpose, too. When you are ready to
speak, you will.

SAPPHO: She has a gift for silencing.

ANACTORIA: She still calls your name in the night.

SAPPHO: She renews her curse under the moon.
    I would be cursed with coldness.
    An icy chill would silence me.
    Both of us could not live, she said,
    and from that day I have not sung.

Like Timas, I am struck dumb.

ANACTORIA: Atthis cursed you from hurt. She wants you back.

SAPPHO: Why? She is Sappho now.
    She is the one who turns
    untouched girls into goddesses,
    rousing an immortal breath
    from inconstant flesh.

    [*Silence. Then, off-stage, we hear* CLEIS *singing one of* SAPPHO's *old songs. She enters, half-intoxicated, bearing a cup of honey drink, an offering to Aphrodite.*]

CLEIS: You know the place: then

    Leave Crete and come to us
    waiting where the grove is
    pleasantest, by precincts

    sacred to you: incense
    smokes on the altar, cold
    streams murmur through the

    apple branches, a young
    rose thicket shades the ground
    and quivering leaves pour

    down deep sleep; in meadows
    where horses have grown sleek
    among spring flowers, dill

    scents the air. Queen! Cyprian!
    fill my gold cup with love
    stirred into clear nectar.[37]

    [*She sets the cup down and looks up.*]

    Ana! What wonderful fruits.
    And look, I have strong honey drink
    borrowed from Sappho's own store.
    Surely the goddess will smile on us.
    Ana, I'm meeting him tonight!

ANACTORIA: Cleis, shssh!

Sappho, I have to go.
Atthis is waiting for me.

[*Exits.*]

CLEIS: Mother! What are you doing here?

SAPPHO: You grow bold on my song and my drink
but shrink from my sight.
Have you become just like them?
Each one has eaten her fill,
then turned in distaste from the used flesh.

CLEIS: You're out of sorts because your lovers are gone.
But that's not my fault. You could have had Ana
for yourself if you'd let me go when I asked. So I
don't care a fig for their loss. I came here with gifts
so the goddess will bless my love for a man.

SAPPHO: Gifts you were given at my knee.

CLEIS: Gifts that will set me free.

[CLEIS *runs out.*]

SAPPHO [*calling after* CLEIS]: Cleis, come back.
Cleis, don't let us fight.

[*Begins to speak as if* CLEIS *were there.*]

Come, sit with me.
I will sing you a song
in praise of your new womanhood.
Come, we'll pick dill and thyme,
then weave the fresh shoots into your hair.
We will enter the cave.
We will stand on her lip and hear the sea's roar.
We will let the sound enter us. We will grow large
with the sound. It was that way when you were born,
that way when you pulled at my breast.
The mystery you must relearn already roots in your flesh.
Two hearts fatally bound become like the ocean's breath,

[83]

wakening first in one, then in the other, self.

[*She looks in the direction* CLEIS *has gone.*]

Cleis, can you understand?
I wanted to tell you these things.
Wanted . . . but that was long ago . . .
when my words had force
and want sometimes answered want.
It is clear now
Atthis's curse cuts me deep.
Wounded far worse than Timas was,
Sappho speaks in a voice no one hears.
Each one forgets the pull of my words.
From such cruel forgetfulness Athena sprang
fullborn from the head of Zeus,
forgetting herself and all of us,
forgetting the motherflesh.

[SAPPHO *puts out the brazier light with her hands.*]

Sappho is dead,
dead to herself.
A siren song
called revenge
lures Sappho's corpse
into hideous realms.

[SAPPHO *exits.* TIMAS *and* CLEIS *enter; they are wrestling. They are dressed in bright, scant clothes wound around their bodies. The two lock into a sitting position, facing each other, legs intertwined.*]

CLEIS: Timas!
    Shssh!
    I'm meeting him tonight!
    He was so mad when I stood him up,
    it's taken me weeks to win him back.

[CLEIS *and* TIMAS *roll to the ground.* CLEIS *kneels above* TIMAS.]

Timas! He's handsome and strong.
He can pick me up with one hand and fling me around.

But tonight he won't need to do that.

[CLEIS *falls on top of* TIMAS, *moving her hips around.*]

What does it feel like, the first time?
I wish you could talk!
Atthis gets angry whenever I ask.
She's just been with women, not once with a man.
It's not the same. What does she know about love?

[TIMAS, *angered and frightened for* CLEIS, *rolls over on top of her and pulls her up, then flips her over her back to the ground.*]

Timas! Why'd you do that?
The mouth of the cave is right here.
I almost fell in.
I could have died.

[CLEIS *gets up.*]

My shoulder is hurt.

[CLEIS *begins walking fast, rubbing her shoulder.* TIMAS *follows behind her, concerned, but* CLEIS *will take no comfort. Then, suddenly, she flops to the ground.* TIMAS *sits down behind her and begins to rub her shoulder, gently.* ATTHIS *and* ANACTORIA *appear, also wrestling. With them it is like a happy dance. They keep moving in and out of beautiful, sensuous poses, their bodies working in simple harmony. They seem perfectly matched.*]

They're awfully good. Remember how clumsy
Anactoria was? Of course, Sappho says you have
to love someone well to wrestle her to the ground.
I'm so mad at her I could shriek. I want her to leave
me alone. She ought to have let you wear the crown.
You deserve a love of your own! It serves Sappho
right that Atthis took Ana away.

[TIMAS *wraps her arms around* CLEIS *and lays her head on her shoulder.* ANACTORIA *and* ATTHIS *are panting hard, laughing, entwined together on the ground.*]

ANACTORIA [*pounding her hand on the ground*]: Finished. Done.
Pinned to the ground.

[85]

Up Atthis. Off of me now.

ATTHIS: Can't.

ANACTORIA: Are you stuck?

ATTHIS: Caught at the core.
   The quake in the cave
   you started last night
   has not stopped.

ANACTORIA: Atthis, get off. I won't let you make love,
   even with words, if I can't move.

[ATTHIS *raises herself up and* ANACTORIA *wriggles free under her, but the two are still entwined.*]

ATTHIS: Last night you straddled me
   and beamed with delight. "Atthis,"
   you cried, "I can't tell where I leave off
   and where you start." And we rolled in the bed
   until we began the entire adventure again.
   "Atthis," you said, as you rolled like the earth
   under my weight, "I am born from your touch. Born
   wholly awake and alive." You fell asleep on my breast.
   Such tenderness overtook me then, I rose to a tender
   release as you lay sleeping there.

ANACTORIA: And you called Sappho's name.

ATTHIS: I did not.

ANACTORIA: I woke to that sound.

ATTHIS: You lay still. You dreamt your worst fear.

ANACTORIA: Or you in your revery spoke
   the wish that must shatter all else.

ATTHIS: Ana, don't torture us.

[*She kisses her.* SAPPHO *enters.*]

ANACTORIA: Sappho, hello.

[CLEIS *decides to punish her mother in front of them all.* SAPPHO *is reserved, holding herself aloof.*]

CLEIS: But it looks like you've missed the match.

SAPPHO: So I have.

CLEIS: Do you want to wrestle with me?

SAPPHO: Can I decide?

CLEIS: Of course. You decide everything else.

SAPPHO: I think you and I have wrestled enough these past weeks.

CLEIS: Perhaps Ana is more to your taste.

ANACTORIA: I'm afraid I'm worn out.

CLEIS: Aptly put, isn't it. Since you refuse Timas her due it means that
　　　Atthis is left.

ATTHIS: Yes, how familiar. But today I decline the honor.

CLEIS: I guess you are out of luck.
　　　No one wants to feel your weight.

SAPPHO: It seems so, doesn't it?
　　　Luck is as fickle as a daughter's love.
　　　Just when it seems at its height,
　　　it can vanish complete. Atthis,
　　　I hope that's not true of the good
　　　fortune I have carried here. This letter
　　　from Sardis just came. I thought it worth-
　　　while to bring it direct, though it may
　　　interrupt the rest of the day you have planned.

[SAPPHO *hands the letter to* ATTHIS.]

ANACTORIA: From Sardis? Do I know who sent it?

SAPPHO: You might know the name.

[ATTHIS *lets out a happy shriek.*]

ATTHIS: My first commission has come! I'm to be paid for my work!

[CLEIS *and* TIMAS *jump with delight.*]

ANACTORIA: Atthis, that's grand!
Can you put me into a verse
and be paid for your happy choice?

ATTHIS: No, silly goose, of course not.
Poets never get paid to write
what we want. Male poets get paid
to write funeral laments for heroes
dead in the wars or to sing praises of
heroes victorious, while women are paid
to write songs for the night other women
are wed: to gravely lament the maidenhead's death and praise the conquering love.

ANACTORIA: Well, it helps your name get around.

ATTHIS: I do it just for the money it brings.
I'll write some doggerel verse of the kind
I've helped Sappho write many times. Once
for some groom especially pompous we even
managed to sing our own praises.

[ATTHIS *enacts both voices.*]

FIRST VOICE: Raise the rafters! Hoist
them higher! Here comes
the bridegroom taller
than Ares!

SECOND VOICE: *Hymenaon!*

[*As* ATTHIS *recites the second verse,* CLEIS *and* TIMAS *pick her up by the legs, so she grows taller.*]

[88]

FIRST VOICE: He towers
    above tall men as
    poets of Lesbos
    over all others!

SECOND VOICE: *Sing Hymen*
    O Hymenaon. [29]

ATTHIS: Oh, we laughed hard making that up.
    He was short as a suckling pig, himself, but he
    was so pleased with our verse he sent us a bonus
    of two baskets of olives, four heads of cheese,
    and some fine Sardinian wine. We threw a feast
    that lasted three days.

SAPPHO: It's also from Sardis that this commission has come.

ANACTORIA [*taking the letter*]: Let me see who asked for the verse.

ATTHIS: Who wants to help me write the rhyme?
    You'll have a share in whatever bonus is sent.
    Let's pretend we have a thin groom and a fat bride;
    then we sing of the width of the globe he has trod
    and of his ravenous love.

CLEIS: Sorry, Atthis, I haven't time. Timas, come. Will you perfume me
    after I've bathed and find some fresh flowers for my hair?

SAPPHO: Cleis, tonight you will study with me.

CLEIS: Catch me, if you can. [*She runs off;* TIMAS *follows.*]

SAPPHO: Ana, you haven't long to learn what I teach. Will you come to my
    room when you finish here?

[*Since reading the letter,* ANACTORIA *has been standing silent.*]

ATTHIS: How dare you say that to her. Especially when everyone knows you
    are blocked. She can't be your muse.

SAPPHO: Perhaps not. But she has served well as yours.

ATTHIS: I'm teaching her to write and to sing
    as well as you taught me,
    but without half the pain.
    You'd toss her away in a year or two.

SAPPHO: I would know when to let her go.
    That's all I knew with you.

ATTHIS: You threw me away when I challenged you.
    Jealousy of my work was all you knew.

SAPPHO: If you are so safe from that fear,
    why won't you let her study with me?

ATTHIS: Why should she drink at a well that is dry?

SAPPHO: Thirst teaches us where water is.

    [SAPPHO *exits.*]

ANACTORIA: You are cruel to her.

ATTHIS: She with her tender tongue
    is cruel as a snake in the grass,
    hissing a song before she strikes.

ANACTORIA: You two have to make up.
    This is your home.
    I will have to go back to mine.

ATTHIS [*covering* ANACTORIA's *mouth with her hand*]:
    Hush, don't even say such a thing.

ANACTORIA: I must, Atthis, because it's the truth.
    I was sent here to learn pride in myself.
    "Enough pride for a lifetime of being a wife,"
    my mother said as she helped me pack. And I have
    learned that . . . from you. But I'll be gone in three
    months, less. I am betrothed, Atthis, you know that.

ATTHIS: So what!
    Betrothed to someone you

have seen once or twice
shaking your father's hand
as they agreed on a price!

ANACTORIA: A noble man, and kind.

ATTHIS: So was the man who sent this commission to me.
I met him at a contest last year. We smiled and spoke.
He said he was taken with my verse and would like me
to be better known. What if he wrote to propose,
would I be so glad to be asked I would leave you
without a thought?

ANACTORIA: It's not the same thing.

ATTHIS: Its exactly the same.
How would you feel
if I left you for a man?

ANACTORIA: Atthis, he and I have the same taste.
He has hired you to write our wedding verse.

ATTHIS: What a hideous joke.

ANACTORIA: Sappho knew it when she brought the letter here.
I've told her his name.

[ATTHIS *grabs the letter from* ANACTORIA's *hand and rips it up.*]

ATTHIS: Sappho did this?

ANACTORIA: That won't help.
I will leave to be wed
and you could use the money
your verses will bring.

ATTHIS: They would ban what I'd write
to the man who has stolen my love.

ANACTORIA: Atthis, please . . .
I was betrothed before I came here.

ATTHIS: Right, you're rich so you're told you
    must reproduce. I'm poor. No one
    troubles me about making an heir.

ANACTORIA: But it happens this way all the time,
    doesn't it? Many girls come here to learn
    what you teach. But most of them leave to be wed.

ATTHIS: When I knelt at your feet and opened you up
    to yourself with my kiss and with my tongue
    let loose your silver life-giving milk, did
    you dare think you were simply receiving your due
    as someone who came to study metre and rhyme?

ANACTORIA: Atthis, please, that's not what I meant.

ATTHIS: When your warmth lured me in, like that cave
    over there lures us down, when I felt your ruby wet self give form to
    each longing I have, don't you think
    I sacrificed distance and fear on that altar of flesh?

ANACTORIA: Atthis, please . . .
    What happened with us isn't a myth.

ATTHIS: What did you hear in that cave
    waiting to rise into my arms?
    A man's voice? Did you promise yourself
    to him after you'd learned how to love?

ANACTORIA: I can't help what I hear.

ATTHIS: Yes you can. Listen to me.
    I am the one whose touch sings through your flesh.

ANACTORIA: You ask for too much.
    It's clear in each image you use.
    Sappho must have felt as I do.

ATTHIS: What did you hear in that cave?
    Sappho's voice laughing at me?
    "Use her," she screamed, "use her,
    then tighten and close like the parched

ground to the root she sent down."
Is that what the cave said?

ANACTORIA: Stop torturing me.

ATTHIS: What did you hear?
   I will know why you turn from this love.

ANACTORIA: But I don't turn from you,
   if I wish to include something else.
   A man and children, perhaps;
   we were made for all this.
   And I can't cut myself off.
   Atthis, listen to me!
   In my dreams, a woman and a man
   both lie in my arms. Through me
   their worlds meet and because
   of them both I am whole. When
   the dream comes I feel like I felt
   when I stood alone in that cave,
   as if at the center point
   where compassion is infinite.

ATTHIS: Take me to Sardis with you.

ANACTORIA: You would suffocate.

ATTHIS: What air will you breathe?
   Respectable talk, his business affairs,
   your children's demands?

ANACTORIA: You don't understand. He is kind.

ATTHIS: Have him come here.
   If he loves you,
   he can make his home
   here with us.

ANACTORIA: He couldn't live here.
   He's a cavalry officer, a hero.

ATTHIS: He is more than a hero

[93]

He is a god in my eyes—
the man who is allowed
to sit beside you—he

who listens intimately
to the sweet murmur of
your voice, the enticing

laughter that makes my own
heart beat fast . . .

ANACTORIA: Atthis, this is unbearable, stop.

ATTHIS: It is Sappho's verse.
How well she understood
the pain you have brought.

            If I meet
you suddenly, I can't

speak—my tongue is broken;
a thin flame runs under
my skin; seeing nothing,

hearing only my own ears
drumming, I drip with sweat;
trembling shakes my body
and I turn paler than
dry grass. At such times
death isn't far from me. [39]

Sappho knows, doesn't she?
Sappho knows what it means to be left.

ANACTORIA: Come, I will take you to her.

ATTHIS: Yes, take me to her.
To her sitting stiff in her chair.
You two can laugh at the creature
who begged for your love
by rolling over on its back.

ANACTORIA: Atthis, come home.

ATTHIS: I am going home

to the cave. To the same
sweet place you run from.
To the cave opening up to the sea.
I am called there by the sea's shout
as she slams her soft flesh into rock.
I will follow the dark to that sound
and dive from the rocks of the cave
onto the rocks the sea hides.
I will let the sea's cold breath
change desire to death.
There is no comfort above
where women lie of their love.
The rank sweet fullness
of death calls me down
I will know consummation
in her arms.

[ATTHIS *rushes into the cave;* ANACTORIA *watches her go, then leaves, running in search of* SAPPHO.]

ANACTORIA: Sappho!

[TIMAS *enters, starts to enter the cave, then hears* CLEIS *weeping and turns back to her.*]

CLEIS: Why am I crying?

Am I still sad
because of my
lost maidenhead? 36

[TIMAS *begins to sing a wordless song, making the sounds in her throat to a poem of* SAPPHO's. CLEIS *listens and begins to sing the words.*]

CLEIS [*as* TIMAS *hums the music to this song*]:

Like a quince-apple
ripening on a top
branch in a tree top

not once noticed by
harvesters or if
not unnoticed, not reached

[95]

Like a hyacinth in
the mountains, trampled
by shepherds until
only a purple stain
remains on the ground. 34

Timas, hush.
Sappho's song tells
a part of the truth.
It happened too fast.
Then he left.
Left me, I felt,
with his soul
awash in my flesh.
What am I to do
with his gift
when I am so
broken and changed
I no longer know
who I am?

[TIMAS *leads* CLEIS *to the rocks next to the cave. She comforts* CLEIS *in her arms. Silence.* SAPPHO *enters.*]

SAPPHO: Is she silent now?
Running, I thought I heard her call
like the eager shy girl who once bade me come to her room.
Then I stood silent a moment or two outside her door
while she gathered courage to call me again
and I, gathering courage, slipped in.
Call to me now and I will come.
Call to me, call.

I will lay my ear to your breast
and drink up the great choral ode, half terror, half joy
that echoed so long in our flesh.
Call to me, call.

[SAPPHO *begins to hear voices, as if in a nightmare: the voices of her conscience, accusing her of the murder she fears she has committed. She hears the angry, taunting voices of the women in her school; especially,* SAPPHO *hears the voice of* TIMAS.]

TIMAS: Did you strangle that cry in her throat?
How can you bring her voice back,
you who have strangled your own?
Your truth grew stonelike and dumb
when you tore her out of your heart.

CLEIS and ANACTORIA: Tore her out of your heart.
Tore her out of your heart.

TIMAS: Sappho has silenced so much.
You are too broken to sing in a voice
full enough to call her back.

CLEIS and ANACTORIA: Too broken to sing.

TIMAS: She is gone from you, gone.
Will you find her mute flesh swollen
among the soft waves? Will you gather
her piece by piece from where she has
shattered against the rock?
Sappho has killed what she loved.
Death is the mask you have worn.
Sappho the goddess of death.
Death-like you enter the wound.
Death-like go back to the spot
where you stalked life.

[*Circling* SAPPHO *while singing,* TIMAS, ANACTORIA *and* CLEIS *dress her in the
death-gown, as she had dressed* ANACTORIA *as Aphrodite in Act I.* SAPPHO *enters the
death-cave, where* ATTHIS *sees her as the figure of Death.*]

ATTHIS [*appearing from behind a cave wall*]: I came alone to Death's house.
There Death is, bidding me come.
How familiar it is; how like the time
I bowed to those other comforting arms.
I had run from my mother's cold house and stood
cold with sweat on her step.
"Come," she said, leading me in.
"Stand where the light wreaths your hair.
Sing me this verse.
Stop shifting about. Sing it again.
Yes, there is music inside.

[97]

You will make your home here with us."

What secret pulse will Death touch?
What song will I learn in Death's arms?

DEATH: Come, lovely child,
   you will grow whole in my house.

ATTHIS: Make me into the vision you have.

DEATH: Give what I ask.

ATTHIS: I am yours to do with as you wish.

DEATH: Give Death her fill from the center of self.
   Sorrow, first.
   Sorrow for what you are,
   for what you hoped to become.
   Sorrow for what is lost.
   Sorrow for all that is past.
   Here, in Death's house, grief stops.
   Find sorrow where it lives and give that grieving flesh to me.

[*Locked in* DEATH's *embrace,* ATTHIS *emits a cry of sorrow.*]

Anger next.
You will come free into my world.
Anger at her who gave you birth,
give that bitter anger up. Anger
at those who birthed you again in their love—
let that gnawing anger go. Anger at those
who betrayed every gift—they were afraid.
Death never fails a needy child.
Give anger to me.

[ATTHIS *struggles with* DEATH; *she lets her anger out in a long cry.*]

Fear.
Fear of loss.
Fear of being alone.
Fear of all you betrayed.
Fear of the cycle itself.

Fear of Death.
You will come open to me,
unencumbered by fear.
Put that stinking thing in my hand.

[ATTHIS *is brought down to the ground by* DEATH; *she gives a long, fearful cry.*]

DEATH: Now desire must end.
    You must want nothing more.
    All is formless where you go.
    You cannot inflict beauty or meaning on Death.
    Put the desire to craft and to make in my hand.

[ATTHIS *struggles to free herself from* DEATH.]

Give what I ask.

ATTHIS: I cannot cut that ache out of my flesh.
    I do not know where it starts.

DEATH: I am ready to take you into my arms
    but cannot
    unless you give desire up.

ATTHIS: [*wrenches away from Death and stands; the fight becomes more even*]:
    If I refuse, what will you do?
    What will you do if I take myself back?
    Will you still be Death in your death-like mask,
    will you breathe death into my face?
    Will you freeze my life with your stone-cold breath,
    wrap my life in your stone-cold arms?
    If I refuse to do what you ask,
    what will become of Death?

DEATH: We are one flesh,
    twinned by a singular need.
    Put the desire to craft and to make
    into my arms. You will rest.

ATTHIS: Mother-death, call me again,
    weave your spell one more time,
    your voice is growing weak.

What will you save me from?
Desire, my own, to throw myself
weeping into your arms.
That is the one desire I disown.

Let me take off your mask.

DEATH: You cannot see me plain.
    You have looked but have not seen.

ATTHIS: I will take off the mask that has kept
    you hidden from me.

DEATH: You wear that mask, not I.

ATTHIS: I faced Death
    and the mask dropped from my eyes.
    Now it will drop from yours.

DEATH: You will ruin the work of the cave.

ATTHIS: No. I complete the action begun.
    I no longer fear Death
    when I feast on the beloved.

[*She lifts the mask from* SAPPHO's *head. She looks into* SAPPHO's *eyes. She feasts on* SAPPHO's *face.*]

Long ago, when bee-like I churned
you to honey under my tongue,
I saw your great composed face
crack apart from pleasure's strain.
How fragile you seemed to me then.
But I never dared speak of those times.
I was afraid. I needed you to be strong.
How fragile you seem to me now.
Let me take off this gown.

[ATTHIS *takes the death-gown off* SAPPHO.]

SAPPHO: Do you dare look into my face?
    I am rotten with Death.

ATTHIS: We were both lost in her arms.

SAPPHO: I followed you here,
    followed you into this cave;
    I would have become whatever you craved.

ATTHIS: That you would come to me . . .
    How often I wished you might have come to me
    as you are; that I might have been strong while
    you lay in my arms and wept at the force of our bond.

SAPPHO [singing ATTHIS's lines]:
    "We have changed desire for death
    into sensations of . . ."
    Have we soured the milk of our love?

ATTHIS: We have mixed it with all that it lacked.

[CLEIS and TIMAS arrive, bearing a bowl of honey.]

CLEIS: Mother, look!
    I have drunk of the honey myself.
    It was wondrous strange.
    First I felt totally changed.
    Now I feel happy and free.
    I can't wait for tonight and
    the same sweet taste in my mouth.

    You two ought to dip in your tongues.
    It's the most irresistible thing.
    Once you begin, you can't stop.

ATTHIS: Cleis, give me the bowl.
    You have grown skilled in its use;
    still you might learn a bit if you watch.

[ATTHIS paints SAPPHO's lips with the honey, and kisses her. The life of the school
returns. CLEIS and TIMAS share a kiss. Only ANACTORIA is not among the group. She
is packing to return to Sardis.]

SAPPHO [to ATTHIS, kissing her]:
    Come with me back

to the light. I am
fertile again and will
sing what Ana cannot.

ANACTORIA [*With her bag on her arm she sings* SAPPHO's *song*]:
   Yes, Atthis, you may be sure

                 Even in Sardis
Anactoria will think often of you
of the life we shared here, when she seemed
the Goddess incarnate
to you and your singing pleased her best

Now among Lydian women she in her
turn stands first as the red-
fingered moon rising at sunset takes

precedence over stars around her;
her light spreads equally
on the salt sea and fields thick with bloom

Delicious dew pours down to freshen
roses, delicate thyme
and blossoming sweet clover; she wanders

aimlessly, thinking of gentle
Atthis, her heart hanging
heavy with longing in her little breast

She shouts aloud, Come! we know it;
thousand-eared night repeats that cry
across the sea shining between us. 40

A MONSTER HAS STOLEN THE SUN

New Cycle Theater at The Arts at St. Ann's presented Act I of *A Monster Has Stolen the Sun* on February 19, 1981. It was directed by Burl Hash, with music composed by Roberta Kosse, setting and lighting by Michael McBride, costumes by Sally J. Lesser and Kathleen Smith. The cast was as follows:

IAN	Richard Davidson
ANGUS	Ruis Woertendyke
ETAIN	Jeanne Morrissey
VINCENT	William Ward
BRIGIT	Mary Krapf
OWAIN	Thomas Kopache
ELEN	Kim Croninger
MACHA	Dolores Brandon
CROW-WOMEN	Barbara Callender
	Lumengo Joy Hooks
	Tyra Liebmann
	Lauri Lowell

The play was presented in its entirety at two rehearsed readings, directed by Florence Stanley, at Smith College in September of 1985, and at Celebrate Brooklyn in November of 1985, produced by New Cycle Theater in association with Celebrate Brooklyn.

CHARACTERS

ANGUS, *a carver*

IAN, *a shepherd*

BRIGIT, *a midwife and healer*

OWAIN, *master of this small kingdom*

ELEN, *daughter of Angus and mistress of Owain*

ETAIN, *Owain's wife; she is pregnant*

VINCENT, *a Christian monk and Etain's confidant*

MACHA, *a woman come down from the high places in the mountains; in Act I she too is pregnant*

DIEDRE, FIOLA, MEENA, CLEEVNA, *peasant weavers and spinners, also* CROW-WOMEN

CONOR, *Owain and Etain's son, age twelve in Act II, sixteen in Act III*

ETAIN, *Macha's daughter, age twelve in Act II, sixteen in Act III*

SETTING

A small settlement at the edge of the sea on an island inhabited by Celtic peoples. The time is the sixth century, roughly the moment of collision between pagan Celt and Christian Celt world-views. The action takes place in the yard in front of the house and outbuildings belonging to Lord Owain; close to the shore; close to the upright stones of the dolmen marking the sacred burial place of Owain's folk; and in the purple mountains rising above. The play spans sixteen years in the lives of the characters.

ACT I

SCENE ONE

[*The winter solstice is being celebrated by an annual fertility ritual intended to call back the sun and to start the gradual lengthening of days leading to spring and the return of growth to the land. Three times the people dance in a winding procession around the four corners of the land they farm for their lord* OWAIN.]

PEOPLE [*singing*]: Each spirit of life bless our calling.
Each daimon who lives in each ridge,
Each spirit of plain and of field,
Bless the need that we have for the sun to return.
Bless the need that we have for the sun to return.

Bless each maiden and youth.
Each woman and tender youngling.
With the fire that passes between them.
Let them call back the light of the sun.
Let them call back the light of the sun.

Bless each goat, sheep and lamb,
Each cow, and horse and pig.
Infuse all the flocks and the herds
With desire to mount, thrust and receive.
With desire to mount, thrust and receive.

Wed our king to the land he walks thrice around.
Let cold winter's chaste cover be softened
Beneath the weight of Lord Owain.
May the earth shift and groan with desire.
May the earth shift and groan with desire.

[OWAIN *is at the head of the processsion. Dancing with him is a young woman named* ELEN, *his mistress of the moment, who is the daughter of* ANGUS, *the carver, the senior and perhaps most authoritative man in the land — he is the director of this ritual and the maker of the ritual masks. As the procession leaves the yard,* ANGUS *appears, carry-*

[107]

ing the rough wooden mask of a puck goat's head. It is comical and grotesque. With him is IAN, *the shepherd.*]

IAN: Off they go, thrice round the fields.
    The proud King Owain with his bright maid,
    your daughter, my friend, I believe?
    It's a sight for starved eyes, a comforting sight,
    for the frost is heavy and the light is short
    and there's no one among us who can say
    if any will live till the first spring day.

ANGUS: Aye, who's to say if Owain himself
    will live to welcome the wheat.

IAN: Don't speak that way, man; you forget
    that the health of the king and the wealth
    of the land are, after all, one and the same.

ANGUS: Are they now, shepherd lad? Do you think so?

IAN: That's what we're here for, isn't it—
    to plead with the spirits of life for return of warmth
    and of growth and renewal of strength for the king?

ANGUS: Aye, that's what we're here for, so some say.
    But it isn't the spirits of earth
    who grant power to the king
    nor he who grants power to them.

IAN: What do you mean?

ANGUS: It's the man who gives actual shape
    to dreams, desires and fears
    who has power over all and might
    make a new king, if he choose.
    Put on this mask I have carved.

IAN: Let me look at it, first.
    Oh, no, I couldn't wear that.

ANGUS: Why not, if I might ask?

IAN: Oh, it's a good piece of work.
  It's carefully made, well wrought.
  But there's something not right.

ANGUS: What do you mean, man, speak up.
  I carved this mask.

IAN: Oh, there's nothing wrong.
  No, not at all.

ANGUS: Well, then, put it on.
  We haven't all day.
  They'll be thrice round the fields in no time at all.

IAN: It's just . . .
  Well, it's not noble or fine.
  It's a bit ugly, if I might say.

ANGUS: It's been crafted with your shape in mind.

IAN: Take it away. I'll act my part
  without a mask. I'm a shepherd, don't forget.
  I know how the puck goats run wild in the hills.

ANGUS: All right. That's where we'll start.
  We'll work from the inside out.
  Show me the fire of the puck goat.

  [IAN *begins to prance and kick his heels in the manner of a wild four-legged thing.*]

  That's grand.
  Kick with a bit more force.
  Out to the side a bit more.

  [IAN *falls while trying to execute the instructions.*]

  Get up, try it again.
  Now bellow a bit, if you can.

  [IAN *lets out a wild bray.*]

  Louder, wilder, if you know what I mean.
  You've been stuck alone up in the hills.
  There's frost on the ground. The days are dark
  and the nights are long. You come down close to the barn.

You smell a soft nanny inside. Bellow, man,
bellow with love and desire.

[IAN *bellows again.*]

Louder, kick higher.
The race of goats will perish from earth
if the puck goat is timid and weak.

[IAN *stops suddenly.*]

Put this on.

[ANGUS *fits the mask on* IAN's *head.*]

You're not who you were.
You're the fertile puck from the mountain tops
come to plant life in a nanny goat.

IAN: Ouch, it's breaking my neck.
    Take it off.
    How can I mount my bride
    bearing the weight of this head?

ANGUS: Stop moaning, now, be still.
    You don't have to mount her at all.
    You just bellow and kick,
    then you're killed. You fall to the ground.
    Be careful to land on your shoulder first.
    Don't hurt the mask. We'll use it again next year.

IAN: What do you mean?
    The whole race of goats demands my seed.

[*He bellows and kicks, dips his head, charges at* ANGUS.]

The nannies line up to receive.
I have to mount each one in turn
or there'll be no milk, no butter, no cheese,
no meat, no flesh without me!

[*More bellows and kicks, again dips his head, charges at* ANGUS.]

ANGUS [*putting his hands on* IAN's *shoulders, holding him at bay*]:
    That's good, puck goat, good.
    We need the one who dares reach deep
    beneath the human face and form

[110]

to touch the beast that no one tames.
We need to slaughter you and drink your blood.

[IAN *stamps his feet and bellows.* BRIGIT, *the midwife, enters.*]

Brigit, look at the god of desire who dies for us all.

BRIGIT: Aye, he is fearsome and grand.

[IAN *lets out a terrible cry of pain, like an animal before the slaughter.*]

Don't be afraid, puck.
I've arnica root to soothe each bruise.
Ignatia to help you return to yourself.

ANGUS: After you've died, she'll give you a potion to make you rise.
The puck goat will revive in a magical way.

BRIGIT: Be brave, puck goat, brave.

ANGUS: You're a thing I've carved from many a shared dream.
You live; the mortal king you battle with will die.

[OWAIN'S *wife,* ETAIN, *enters. She is very pregnant. She comes with* VINCENT, *the monk.*]

Use your fancy, man. Use your mind.
Bellow and kick. Hundreds have gathered to watch,
including the wife of Lord Owain, herself.
You are for each what they long to become,
the force that brings life from death.

[IAN *bellows and kicks.*]

Go, puck, go. Run after the king.
Kick dirt in his face.

[IAN *goes out, following the sound of the procession.* ANGUS *and* BRIGIT *follow.*]

VINCENT: This is a custom I am long revolted by.
The calling up of their false gods,
the way they idolize their thirst for blood and sex.

ETAIN: It's not their rite I tremble at, it is the fact
their king has used me as he'll use that puck,
a thing to conquer and disarm;

[111]

or as he used the fields beneath his feet,
a thing to trample on, a thing to plant;
or as he'll use that girl who clings now to his arm,
a thing to wonder at and to destroy.

VINCENT: The pagan carver with his pagan masks
  has evoked this bloody lust; you can win Lord Owain back.

ETAIN: I can't. The pagan carver raised him from a boy.
  Now his daughter throws herself at him.
  The pagan carver looks with jealous eyes.
  He sees his own weakness, age and death
  smiling from my husband's smiling face.

[IAN *prances in at the head of the procession.* OWAIN, ELEN, ANGUS, BRIGIT *and* THE
PEOPLE *follow.*]

PEOPLE: The puck, the puck,
  let Lord Owain slay the puck.
  We will drink the blood rushing with seed.
  We will pour fruited blood on the earth.
  The wedding will then be complete.

ANGUS [*offering* OWAIN *a sword*]: My Lord, this is a weapon I have crafted
  through long nights alone before a single flame.
  I know it to contain a potent force
  undreamed by lesser men. The weapon
  will release the puck goat's blood
  which fertile potion will call back the sun.

OWAIN: My aged friend, I take your sword with thanks.
  It is an instrument I am glad to have.

[*He turns to* BRIGIT.]

Now I kneel at the feet of one whose ancient
power is unseen yet who evokes a magic strength
in every man. Brigit, bless my quest.

BRIGIT: The blessing asked, it is received.
  Fight well for the sun's return.

[OWAIN *stands and goes to* IAN, *the puck, whom two people have been holding.*]

[112]

OWAIN: Are you ready, puck, to die for life?

[IAN *lets out a bellow. At this moment an eerie purplish light falls across the space and a huge shadow, having the outlines of a great beast, appears. It is an eclipse of the sun. Suddenly, the play battle gives way to a real sense of terror and dread.*]

ANGUS [*in fear*]: A monster has stolen the sun!

BRIGIT: It is tall as the mountain is tall.

ELEN: It is winged and horned.

ANGUS: Chase the creature of death from the land.

[THE PEOPLE *use their instruments to make a loud, cacophonous noise.*]

IAN: Help, ho, what is wrong? I can't see.

FIOLA: Pieces of flesh fall from its wings.

MEENA: It is made of decay and of death.

ANGUS: Chase the monster away who has stolen the sun.

[*He begins to beat* IAN *with his tambourine.*]

IAN: Help. Help. It is evil itself.

[*He stumbles around the space.* THE PEOPLE *chase him, beating him and making noise to scare the "beast" away.*]

VINCENT [*to* ETAIN]: Call him to your side;
you're soon to be the mother of his child.

ETAIN: My Lord . . .

OWAIN: Etain, come. Join with those who tend the land.
They grow wild at the thought a monster has stolen the sun.
Their fear of winter's darkness must be overcome.

BRIGIT [*tossing a tambourine to* OWAIN]: Owain, Etain, come.

[113]

ETAIN: Stay by my side. The loss of the sun and their
  thunderous noise frightens the child in my womb.

ANGUS: Chase the omen of death from the land.

ETAIN: Owain, stay. The sky grows darker and I tremble
  at the madness in the air. I am close to my time.

OWAIN: Join your fear with theirs.
  They do not fear possession by the thing they fear
  but enter in a wild dance with the unknown.

ETAIN: The child feels dead against my flesh.
  Owain, stay.

BRIGIT: Etain, flaunt your ripened self at death.
  Owain, come, I've never called you when you disobeyed.

[OWAIN *joins the crowd.*]

ANGUS: Chase the creature of death from the land.

ETAIN: It is a godless noise they make
  and godless words they speak.
  Go, then, my godless man, run wild
  with the wild pack.

[BRIGIT, ELEN, OWAIN *and all chase* IAN *out of the space, making a loud noise and calling upon the beast to give up the sun.*]

VINCENT [*helping* ETAIN *get down on her knees*]:
  We can outlast their madness with our prayer.
  Some say the moon eclipsed the sun the day
  our Lord was born. Let this be a portent for your babe.
  From the dark hole carved into the sky
  heaven's light appears.

ETAIN: An old woman, toothless and bent, stirs his desire
  more than I who have grown misshapen and large
  bearing the weight of his child.

VINCENT: Lacking God as he does, he weakens from

[114]

a wild woman's call.
She was his midwife and his nurse.
She holds him taut within her grasp.

ETAIN: And I, who hold his future here,
am more to be feared.

VINCENT: You are the temptress who stole his seed.
The old one, the mother who renews.

ETAIN: Growing round I have become the monster
who eats up the sun. I am the dragon shape
he must escape. So he hides himself between
the virgin flatness of his maid and sterile
wisdom of the crone.

[*The light returns to normal. The people are heard playing a simple tune of joy on flutes
and stringed instruments. They wander back into the space.*]

BRIGIT: Etain, I called for you and Owain both.
I did not mean to set my lure against your own.

ETAIN: He has made his choice.

OWAIN [*entering with* ELEN, *he approaches* ETAIN]: See, it is done.
The sun regains its dominance.
Knowing that the light returns
our people better face the long,
dark wait till spring.
So it is with us, Etain,
if you can but trust my monstrous
heart, nothing will end.

[ANGUS *and* IAN *enter.* IAN *carries the puck's head.* ANGUS *and he pass a wineskin
between them.*]

ETAIN: My Lord, I am close to my time.
I am overcome by thoughts
I would have freedom from.
I am not at ease surrounded by a crowd
who makes our business theirs.

[115]

[*to* VINCENT]

Take me into the house; I must rest.

[*As they start to exit, the sound of the crow is heard.*]

BRIGIT: Come, Owain, we will follow the call of that crow.
  I am full of mysterious things
  I would have you know.

[*As they are leaving,* ELEN *approaches.*]

ELEN: Owain, take me with you.

OWAIN: I am called by the voice of the crow
  to go where the crow's voice leads.
  Elen, leave me go.
  Look to your work, now, everyone.
  Angus, I would have the harnesses made and the wheels
  repaired by tomorrow morn. Women, I would have all
  of the old wool spun before the child is born.
  Shepherd, since you're here, I would set you
  to cleaning the barn.

[BRIGIT *and* OWAIN *go. All but* IAN, ANGUS *and* ELEN *drift away to work.*]

IAN: Say, carver, and carver's daughter,
  all is not well between the lord and his lady.
  So he runs off with Brigit the seer and dumps all his
  wrath on the poor. Sure what else does he keep us for?
  The lords and ladies could work as well as we, but then
  they'd have no one to blame for the sorrows they cause
  and no one to look down on when they feel bad.

ANGUS: Elen, are you ill?

ELEN: What makes you ask?

ANGUS: Didn't you hear the shepherd just say all is not well
  between the lord and his lady. Are you sick, girl?

ELEN: I'm fine, father, fine.

ANGUS: There you are, shepherd, you've heard the girl answer:
 All is well between the lord and his lady. All is plump,
 young and healthy that has come between the lord and his lady.

ELEN: Stop. Will you let me alone.
 I'm tired from all that has passed.
 I don't want to hear your wagging tongue.

ANGUS: Tired, eh. Something could have happened to you I
 never allowed. Do you sit there and mope because a seed
 in your belly turns you sickly and weak?

ELEN: Leave me alone.

IAN [who has been standing about uncomfortably the whole time]:
 Uh, that's just what I thought I'd do.
 My flock must be scattered all over the mountain.
 Here's your head back, carver. I acted my part quite well,
 don't you think? It's all left me with much to consider.
 But my own wife's with child and close to her time to deliver.

 [He leaves.]

ANGUS: Even that simpleton spills his seed into fertile
 ground, while I go in shame since you've gone,
 catching my seed in my hand.

ELEN: Your talk makes me sick.

ANGUS: When I spoke praise to your perfect fingers
 and slender toes you loved to hear me talk.
 You loved to lie in my arms smiling up at my words.
 I could have sired your child, but I held myself back.
 I could have kept you for mine, but I let you go to a lord
 who favored you for a month, then left you without a word.

ELEN: No man could use me more ill than you have done.

ANGUS: Elen, no man will ever love you as I do to this day.
 No man's love could begin as mine did.

ELEN: I've work to do.

[117]

I've no time to listen to you.

[*She turns to go; he stops her.*]

ANGUS: Your mother died the hour you were born.
Brigit, weeping, gave you to my arms.
I was a lad, the girl I loved had died.
I paced the fields and ridges, cradling you in my arms.
I keened my grief to all life's living things.
One by one they each gave back a call: "Joy, joy, joy,"
the sea birds and the wood birds sang. "Joy for what you
cradle in your arms." "Joy," called the wave that
pounded on the shore. "Joy," the bitter wind replied.
I keened my grief aloud. All life answered, "Joy."
"You hold what matters now within your arms. Joy for what
endures past death." You turned your face into my breast.
I sat down upon a rocky ledge and let the waves repeat
the thunderous call. "Joy for what is," they beat against
the shore. I rocked you gently in my arms.
I never loved a woman, child, better than I have loved you.

ELEN: I was your daughter, not your concubine or wife.

ANGUS: I loved you, Elen, what else could I do?

ELEN: Your love is vile. It has always been. All my growing
years I trembled when I heard you come.
You forced yourself on me, but now I'm grown.
Sit there like a withered branch.
Stare down at the ugly head you made
and think what you have meant by love.

[*She exits.*]

ANGUS: Because I treated you as if you were a queen
you turn on me in scorn when you are grown.
I would have loved you better, if I could.
I cared for you the only way I knew.

SCENE TWO

[BRIGIT *and* OWAIN *approach the ancient burial spot, which is marked by a dolmen, rising out of the rocks.*]

BRIGIT: Once I carried you, slung between my breasts
and danced here through the night.
Now the rocks pierce the soles of my feet
and the wind reminds me of death.

OWAIN: Once we danced together in this spot,
our breath billowing up.
We were the crystal waves that leapt
from the depths of the sea
to shatter in brilliant shapes
for the sake of eternity.

BRIGIT: This much we know, but much is lost,
so I have brought you here as if to dream
the future of some unbegotten race.
This much is known, and not much else:
how I caught you from your mother's heaving womb
to bear you at my breast. How you stood
shaking with desire when I aroused your sex,
then journeyed to the center of the earth
to spill your virgin seed into that whirling space.
How life and death seemed one to you that once.
All this is known, but nothing else,
so I have brought you here as if to dream
the future of an unbegotten race.

OWAIN: Once I knelt in awe before your shape.

[*He kneels.*]

I stared at the weight and motion of your breasts
and felt my own shape change.

BRIGIT: Now a passage into yet another form is asked.
The hungry child sucking at my breast,

the long-haired youth delighting in the dance
have grown into a man whose time to father
the unknown is come.

OWAIN: Is Etain already due?
    These months have seen me turn from her.

BRIGIT: I have watched. I have not said a word.
    Etain kneels in prayer on the cold stones;
    she follows the bird's flight with her eyes.

OWAIN: Etain grew large and quiet and unknown before my sight;
    so I turned from what I could not understand.

BRIGIT: And sought a new love out.

OWAIN: As you sought me when you, too, felt a need
    to bond with something vibrant and untouched.

BRIGIT: I have watched and have not said a word.

OWAIN: Did you know a charm that would
    have kept my love for her alive?

BRIGIT: Three things only do I know:
    the love of the moment we cherish and keep;
    the love of what was and will never come back;
    the torturous love of the unborn.
    This last I would share with you.

OWAIN: Come to me for one instant out of time.
    Let us be once more as we were,
    a girlish youth gasping with wonder
    and the wise woman he lay under.

BRIGIT: Back, further back in your heart,
    search for what was and has been forgot.

OWAIN: Take me back beyond that midnight spring
    when the moon lay open and full
    to a time I lay snug in your arms
    and the world was an orb of milk-like flesh

[120]

and milky smells.

BRIGIT: Back, further back in your heart.
   Back beyond time or regret.
   You will lend your flesh and your bones
   to the greed of what is unborn.

[OWAIN *squats on the ground. Entranced by* BRIGIT, *he feels himself to be pregnant and he begins to be aware of his growing belly, his ripe heaviness. Completing the spell,* BRIGIT *sings the song of the solitary birth. The crow-women emerge from behind the dolmen to sing with her. They hover around* OWAIN. OWAIN *grows round and heavy, as* BRIGIT *sings. His labor pains begin, and he works to deliver the "child," finally easing it out from between his legs and biting the umbilical cord.*]

On a wind-swept hill on a mountain plain
washed by the salt of the sea and the rain,
a solitary creature—deer, cow, pig, mare, goat,
woman alone—squatted down to give birth.
How many times has this story been told,
how few the listeners? How many times
has the labor been made to the sound
of the wind and the song of the birds?
She who brought forth the unknown,
how many times did she shiver and shake,
caught in the moment of birth, the effort that knows
one release, form out of form, fear raising love?
When the lonely work was done, when she had licked
the infant clean, who was there on that lonely plain
to marvel at what had been made? A bandy-legged calf,
a sniveling runt, an unwanted puck, a son to be feared,
a daughter scorned. The lonely one and the work
of her heart rage at the welcoming wind.

[OWAIN *wakes. He sees the "babe" he has birthed. He cradles and welcomes the "child."*]

OWAIN: Hello, little babe, little beast, little one.
   Where have you been? Where have you come from?
   A moment before you were only the faith
   that the effort would end and a child would be born.
   Your wet head slithers across my chest.
   Your fingers grasp at my flesh.

Your eyes blink open and stare.
You are life looking up, crawling up out of your well.
You have come from the mud, from the ocean's dark you have come,
a beast flung down from the sky, spewed from the lava foam.
How did you dare to trust a love I never have known
would anchor your heart in my own?

[OWAIN *rocks the child, when suddenly the crows begin to caw.*]

What is that sound? The crowd, the world
that calls me from the task of birth. Away,
away, I am not weak. I have not sacrificed my strength.
Away, away you flat-beaked crows.
Stop your screeching, jeering song.

[*He throws the "child" against the rocks, and in a fury chases the birds.*]

Begone you evil tribe of birds.
Begone, you stinking, ugly things,
dead image of an unlived life, away.
Leave me as I was,
a man whose mute and shuttered loins
hold fast against unknown, unwanted things.

BRIGIT: Hush, Owain, hush. Before the rage
which is all you can remember now
lived an image barely touched, inside you still.
Owain, awake, you have been to the source,
turned and fled, but the source of that devouring
delight will one day claim you for her own.
Not the birth, but love of the birth,
not the child, but awe of the child,
not the effort, but reverence before it,
are yours.

[*The dawn has come. A bird's song is heard and* MACHA *answers it. She is seen in the distance, heavy with child. A young lamb is slung across her back. She leaps across the rocks.*]

OWAIN: Who is that?

BRIGIT: It is Macha, the poor shepherd's wife.

OWAIN: She strides with the grace of the wind or the wave

yet her belly is heavy with child.

BRIGIT: She is half-tamed.
　　　She sings with the wildest of birds.
　　　She runs with the hind and the fox.

OWAIN: Why have I not seen her before?

BRIGIT: Her strength bids her keep to herself.

OWAIN: Where is she from? She is not of this place.

BRIGIT: She came down from the mountain last year
　　　to ease the poor shepherd who lived alone.
　　　She grew fond of the one she had found;
　　　now she carries a child under her heart.
　　　Come, the dawn has played itself out.
　　　Macha is gone from our sight. I am called
　　　by the light of the sun back to the tasks of the day.

OWAIN: Go by yourself back to the house.
　　　I would seek out that poor shepherd's flock.

SCENE THREE

[ETAIN *and* BROTHER VINCENT *are walking in the yard, in front of the house. They hear the cry* MACHA *has made as she runs down to the barn with the lamb.*]

ETAIN: Hush, do you hear? Can you see where the wild bird has flown? Where has the wild thing gone? Alone out from the shore, flaunting its delicate strength, dipping a silver wing toward certain death in the waves, soaring up, risking death in the wind. Where has the wild thing gone? Why has it left me alone?

VINCENT: Hush, Etain, hush. The bird will return;
　　　I can chart its flight in your eyes.
　　　The bird will return to sing
　　　at the birth of your child.

[123]

ETAIN: Why does that cry turn sour in my dreams;
      why does death haunt me so, if I am sheltered,
      as you say, sheltered by merciful God?

VINCENT: Etain, kneel down.
      We will pray for that bird's return.

ETAIN: I dreamt last night of that cry, turned terrible and cold.
      I dreamt of the carrion crow
      that picks out the eyes of the new-born lambs
      and leaves the sheep wild in the pasture below.
      I dreamt of a screaming crow, lodged in my womb,
      eating my flesh. I could not dislodge that bird.
      Now it returns, mocking me with its call,
      its beak driven deep, as if I am nailed to it.

VINCENT: You can dislodge that bird with a thought,
      banish it, send it away, make it a creature of day.
      I have heard of a kind of bird
      where the female lays the eggs,
      then the male sits on them. The male bird
      hatches the young, feeds and cares for them.

ETAIN: You would like that, Brother Vincent.

VINCENT: I would. How better could a day's prayers
      be brought to an end than by the furious pecking
      at my backside of the new-born crying for food.

ETAIN: My eggs safe in your nest, I would fly
      out over the sea, spiralling up in a dance,
      to the island beyond the waves where all are
      lovely and young and no death comes.
      If only we were those birds.

VINCENT: God has made us as we are.

ETAIN: Are we not bound by our forms
      to duties we each would disown?

VINCENT: We are made for the work of our Lord.

[MACHA *enters, heavy with child, the small lamb slung across her back.*]

MACHA: I would just go into the barn. I have brought down a lamb born too late in the year to survive to a withered old ewe who is dry. I would just go into the barn and find a warm teat for its mouth.

[*Exits.*]

ETAIN: Who is that?
    She carries a lamb
    from the hills on her back
    as simply as she carries her child.

VINCENT: A poor shepherd's wife,
    grown strong from a hard, dull life.

ETAIN: Leave me, Brother Vincent, our prayers are done.

VINCENT: You should not be left alone in the cold morning air
    and your time so close.

ETAIN: Leave me. I will speak to the one in the barn.

VINCENT: What would you say to her who's never been near the mass, who scorns the sacraments? What would she say to you but foolishness?

ETAIN: The will of a woman heavy with child should not be crossed or the child will be born hair-lipped with a club foot and the good milk will sour in its mouth.

[*She sees* MACHA *by the barn door.*]

Woman, isn't this so?

MACHA: I have heard that to cross a woman heavy with child is to bring a long curse on the house.

VINCENT: Enough of this talk. Come with me, now.

ETAIN: A few minutes alone, Brother Vincent; go. My time is near. I won't be out again in the air.

[*He goes. There is silence between the two pregnant women.*]

ETAIN: You are a shepherd's wife?

MACHA: I tend sheep, lambs and goats.

ETAIN: You carry a shepherd's child?

MACHA: I carry the child I have desired.

ETAIN: Where are you from?

MACHA: The blue mountain risen there under the sun.

ETAIN: You walked to the plain with a lamb on your back
    and your belly full of a child.

MACHA: I walked and I ran.
    I rested myself in the morning sun.
    The beat of the heart of the lamb
    and the beat of the heart of this beast
    who's unborn were like a great song in the world.

ETAIN: What made you come?

MACHA: There's frost in the hills. A lamb born
    this late in the year wouldn't live with
    a ewe too old to nurse.

ETAIN: So you left your bed and your hearth
    to carry a lamb to the barn on your back?

MACHA: I am called by the sound of the sea
    as the wave inside myself breaks.
    I wished to come down to the shore.
    The lamb's need was only my own.
    Don't you feel the same desire
    to squat by the ocean's gate
    and, one with the endless tide,
    deliver what you have made?

ETAIN: I feel no desire at all
    but to be free of this weight.

MACHA [*approaching her*]: Yes, it is time.
 Has your belly been rubbed by someone
 who sees the beauty that weight
 brings to your bearing and to your face?

ETAIN: I have kept to myself
 these changing months.
 I have not wanted to be touched.

MACHA: Sit by my side.
 I will trace the lines of your child
 with my hands. I will draw on your silken flesh
 the beauty of what you have made.

 [ETAIN *sits next to her.* MACHA *begins to rub her stomach. She feels about, high up and
 to one side.*]

 Here are limbs, stretching themselves
 in the golden warmth of the womb.

 [*She feels lower down.*]

 Here, the head, being brave,
 already pointed at the earth.

 [*She lays her head on* ETAIN's *stomach.*]

 And the heart, bold and strong.
 What a fine child you've grown.

ETAIN: Is it ready to be born?

MACHA: Soon, very soon. A day or two or a week.
 It's something we do not know—why the birth
 starts and when, what dream the child dreams
 in that sheltered spot that pushes it out toward life.

ETAIN: Will it be a boy or a girl?

MACHA: I would guess from your shape and the sound
 of the heart you carry a son.

ETAIN: You carry a daughter, then.

MACHA: How do you know?

[127]

[ETAIN *reaches to* MACHA's *stomach now and traces her child as she speaks.*]

ETAIN: Why, someday, when they are grown
    these two can bring forth their own.
    They would make a child of ours,
    as if we had coupled here in the sun
    and left a delicate sprout, conceived
    by a touch and a wish.

MACHA: Soon we will sit side by side at the shore
    bound by our babes; wedded by them we will
    sit, smiling at dreams that well up
    in the silver spray of the waves,
    entranced by the life we have made.

ETAIN: Perhaps all will be as you say.
    Tell me of the birth of the lamb.

MACHA: The sun was trapped by the moon
    when I heard the ewe call.
    I sat in that purple light
    rubbing her warm belly with my hand.
    Sometimes she would turn to look in my eyes
    and I'd answer her look with my own.
    Then she began.

ETAIN: Did she cry out in pain?

[*As* MACHA *speaks,* ETAIN *rises onto all fours. She becomes like the ewe, totally involved in the birth effort, animal-like, and she experiences, for a moment, all of the fire, the pride and the brute force that might have been hers.*]

MACHA: She dug her feet into the earth.
    She hunched and her belly grew tight with each push.
    She parted her lips and her breath gave rise
    to the song of the birth.

[MACHA *sings and she supports* ETAIN's *effort.*]

Five months, little lamb, I have carried you under my heart.
Five months, little lamb, you have weighted me close to the earth.
Each step that I took was echoed by your shifting weight.
Each fright found a place deep inside me; each joy that I had

was silently shared. Drop down, little lamb, you have lived
for five months in my darkness. There has been nothing between us
but trust. Drop down, little lamb, for the time of not knowing
is ended. What has fashioned itself of my flesh must be claimed
by the sun and the wind.

[ETAIN *pushes, as if she were the ewe, completely animal in her effort. She makes the
grunting, groaning cry of birth, delivers the lamb and rests.*]

As the light came back to the sky, she leaned back
her head and smiled. She smiled as if she knew effort
is love and death must lose in the end. She nudged
the lamb up on its feet. It stumbled and grabbed
at her teat.

ETAIN [*She is herself again*]: It was as simple as that.
    As if she were wind or wave,
    and joyously proud in her pain.

MACHA: It was as simple as it seemed.
    All her sorrow was yet to come.
    But that's a tale for another morn.

ETAIN: The ewe died from the birth.

MACHA: She did not.

ETAIN: She died from the effort she made,
    died from the thing she had done,
    died from the force of her cry.

MACHA: The ewe lives as sure as the lamb.
    The birth was well done.

ETAIN: How did you come by that lamb?
    Did you steal the babe she had birthed?
    Did you take away what she loved?
    Did you punish the ewe for the wildness she knew?

MACHA: What trickled out of her teat was yellowed, sour old milk.
    The lamb took one drink and cried.
    It bleated its hunger up to the sky. The ewe shrieked with

anger and fear. She could not feed the thing she'd birthed.
She rushed at the cowering lamb. She kicked, she bit,
she yelled. I picked up the poor turned-on thing. I slung
the lamb over my back.

ETAIN [*singing the song of the bereaved ewe, becoming as she sings, that animal once more,
wild with grief this time, tossing her head. But by the end of the song she is once more
passive and resigned*]:
What I bore in my belly with fear
she bears on her back with pride.
The woman strides off with all that I am;
she leaves me with nothing at all.
What does she care that I hated the weight
of the unborn thing deep in myself
yet bore that brutal desire
in silence, as if it were pride.
What does she care that I shattered myself
and poured my blood out on the earth.
She steals all I have birthed.
What does she care that the effort I made
was more than I could endure, that the cry
that stuck in my throat was the cry of the carrion
bird and all I had dreamed of or hoped devoured
itself in that cry.

[*A loud and terrible scream is heard.* ETAIN *flinches.* MACHA *goes to her.* ETAIN *draws
back.*]

MACHA: It is but the aching branch of an old tree
falling away under the weight of the frost.

ETAIN: It is nothing with form. It is something that has
not been.

MACHA: It is but rocks resettling, or the earth shifting.

ETAIN: Do not lie. It is grief.

MACHA: It is over and gone.

ETAIN: It will return.

MACHA: No, it has fled.

ETAIN: It is sorrow. It will come again.

MACHA: It was a moment out of time. It is gone.

[*The sound comes again. It is a crying in* ETAIN's *womb.*]

ETAIN: It is the child in my womb.

MACHA: It is yourself. Do not fear.

ETAIN: It is the babe, crying for comfort it has not had.

MACHA: Sing, Etain, sing. Not of the pitiful ewe.
Sing songs of comfort for all that must live.

ETAIN: Stop torturing me with your strength.
You mock at my need.
You deny that a woman is frightened and weak.
Go. Leave me alone. The child cries in the womb.
There is nothing to do. He knows me better than you.

[*The cry comes again.* VINCENT *enters.*]

VINCENT: What is that sound?

[BRIGIT *enters from the other side.*]

BRIGIT: Why is there crying in the womb?

ETAIN: She has taken all that I am.

MACHA: I take nothing I would not return.

VINCENT: What evil have you practiced in this place? Even as she weakens,
you grow strong.

MACHA: I am just who I am.

ETAIN: You feed yourself from my form.

[131]

VINCENT: Come, Etain, into the house. We will pray. You'll soon be yourself. Midwife, follow us. Shepherdess, go from this place.

[VINCENT *and* ETAIN *exit.*]

MACHA: You are her midwife, yet you've let her grow crazed with fear. Shame on you, woman, shame. Did you hold her in your arms? Did you rock her to sleep? Did you call her "goddess of life," "giantess with two hearts"? Did you rejoice in her strength, or pride her on her size? Did you sing to her, laugh with her, cry? Did you stand silent in awe at the miracle she will unfold? You have done none of these things. When the pain comes that rips her in two, midwife, what cure will you have? Will you drug her with herbs so she will not learn of her glorious strength? Will you rip the babe from her unwilling flesh, force it to drink at her breast, then smile your superior smile to yourself?

BRIGIT: Wild woman, why have you come down from the hills to ruin the peace of this place? Go back where you've been these many years. Go back to sleep under the rocks.

MACHA: I've come, for the women on this land have grown soft and the men have grown hard. I've come to ask, why? Why have you turned from a woman in need, midwife, why?

BRIGIT: She is not of this land.
She came with the monk on her arm.
She would listen to nothing I said.
It was she took my power away.
Even you in your rage have not the strength
to bring back a power that is feared.
Go away back to your flock,
away from this house.
I will go to Etain and do what I can.

SCENE FOUR

[OWAIN *comes upon* IAN *where he is tending the flock.*]

IAN [*singing*]: The morning brings the sun.
    The night is long.
    The morning brings the sun.
    The sheep and the shepherd are glad.
    All fear of the darkness is gone
    and has fled. The morning has brought
    back the sun. The dark and the cold
    are beaten back by the sun.

OWAIN: There sits a happy man.

IAN: Tired and cold from a long night alone
    but pleased at the sight of the sun.
    Will you share food fit for a king?
    There's a spring with clear water.
    My wife's bread is equalled by no other.

OWAIN: You bid me good welcome to this spot.
    Where is your wife?

IAN: She has run off with a lamb on her back.
    She will return before night.
    She is swifter than wind.

OWAIN: A boast like that ill fits an honest man.

IAN: I speak only the truth.
    Though she carries my child in her womb,
    and has slung a young lamb on her back,
    she runs with the grace of the hind
    and the speed of the morning light.

OWAIN: You mock me with your boast.
    No man has a wife as swift as the woman you describe.

IAN: I speak only the truth. No lie could out-distance my wife.

OWAIN: How did you find such a mate?

IAN: Ah, that is the strangest tale there is.
    One day when the evening sky was dressed in gold, in red,
    in purple, vermillion and blue, she stood at my door.

Clothed in the rays of the setting sun, wrapped in a
mantle of shimmering hair, she seemed an image of a lost
race when people were taller and grander than now
and lived to a hundred or more, when wisdom and wonderful
songs flew like hurrying flocks from their tongues
ruffling the air. She stood silent and proud at my door.
She entered the hut, bringing with her the glorious light.
The hut seemed to grow grand, like a crystal castle
set next to a bubbling stream. She graced it like
an ancient queen. From that day to this she has
lived in my house and not a harsh word have we spoken
or thought. I asked her once as she lay by my side why
she sought me instead of a king. She turned her head
toward the moon, smiled and said, "The moon, the wind,
the sun, the sea and my self; this house, the flock
and a tender touch are finer than riches to me." From
that one wondrous night a child has begun to take form.
And she, who carries the load, becomes swifter, wiser,
more proud and fairer than ever before. Now her smile
itself is like light; she leaps with the hind on the rocks,
answers the birds with her songs, and cradles the ewes in her arms.

OWAIN: You are a victim of love. Your love makes you lie.
No mortal woman has half the virtues you describe.

IAN: On my honor as an honest man, I have not yet begun to praise her.

OWAIN: No woman with child is swifter than a hind.
No woman with child is as proud.
I have seen them grow weak, teary-eyed, lumbering and slow.
No woman with child races the wind.

IAN: No woman but this one woman, perhaps, and she an image of all the
pride and the strength that is past.

OWAIN: You anger me with your boasts. I would have you be quiet or prove
what you say.

IAN: Sit with me through the day; at evening you'll see her return. You'll
learn of her speed, her silver tongue and the courage with which she
carries her young.

OWAIN: You make her sound braver than any man.

IAN: That may well be. For I've not heard the tale that equals her own.

OWAIN: You will prove what you say.

IAN: One look at her glorious self will make my words weak.
　　She can out-wrestle any man and not lose the smile on her face.

OWAIN: There is no man alive who can out-wrestle me.

IAN: No man, perhaps, Lord. No man, at all.

OWAIN: And no shepherd's wife.

IAN: Oh, yes, Sire, she can. But as she's with child, I wouldn't allow it.

OWAIN: Man, I will wrestle your wife
　　or string you up by your hair on a tree,
　　sever your head from your limbs and let your
　　mouth hang open to mock your boast.

IAN: Lord, surely you jest.

OWAIN: I will wrestle the woman you claim as your wife.

IAN: Who *is* my wife, Lord.
　　It's my child inside her.
　　For the sake of the unborn, Sire, let the match
　　be put off until she delivers.

OWAIN: The match will take place as soon as we find her,
　　or you will not live until dinner.

IAN: Lord, please, you frighten a man who's done well in your service. This
　　flock is healthy and large. My tribute is always fully paid.

OWAIN: How do you know the seed she carries is yours?
　　How close to her have you actually been?

IAN: Closer than any man since she came to this land.
　　Closer yet than I am to my death, is that not so, Sire?

[135]

OWAIN: That is for you to consider.
    A woman who's swifter than wind, stronger than men,
    carries no child of a shepherd inside her;
    the soul of a shepherd lodged under her heart
    would make her docile and meek. She would
    grow cow-like and dumb if she carried your son.

IAN: Yes, Sire, yes. Let's forget about me and my wife.
    She's most apt to be snoring right now under some tree,
    the flies buzzing thick round her puffed-out eyes,
    licking the sweet drool from her mouth.

OWAIN: Your boasts ring in my ears.
    Though I asked you to stop, you could not.
    I have seen the woman you describe; though I would
    not fain call her your wife, I will wrestle her
    for your life. Come. We will seek her out
    where she hides.

    [OWAIN *takes* IAN *by the arm and leads him off.*]

SCENE FIVE

    [*In the yard outside* LORD OWAIN's *house.* ELEN *sits, honing an ax.*]

ELEN [*singing*]: O, the blood that waters the ground
    will grow the red poppies and dark violets.

    O, the blood that waters the ground
    will grow up a garden from dust and from rock.
    O, the blood, the red blood that falls from your wounds
    will wash the earth clear of the crimes
    I've whispered to no one, year after year;
    I've whispered to no one, for no one could hear.

    O, the blood from your neck that waters the earth
    will fall like rain on the stalk. All that has frozen
    and died will grow fresh in the balm of your blood.
    The blood, the warm blood will bring back the spring

and wash the earth clean of the crimes
I've whispered to no one year after year;
I've whispered to no one, for no one could hear.

[BRIGIT *enters with a basket of herbs.*]

BRIGIT: Elen, has Owain gone into the house?

ELEN: No one has cast a shadow on the step since the sun came up.

BRIGIT: Pah! [*She spits.*] Run away, with his wife in such terror and pain she
will not open herself to let the babe be born.

ELEN: Is she going to die?

BRIGIT: That I can't tell. I've ergot and rue. Each will help push the child out
of the womb. But I haven't found the fungus or herb that will give her
desire to live.

ELEN: Brigit, I had to do what I did. I had to take Owain for mine.

BRIGIT: Aye, he's handsome and strong. You're lovely and young. No
woman knows till it happens to her the pain of a faithless man.

ELEN: If all that had happened to me was to be left by a man,
you wouldn't see me honing an ax to sever his head.
Owain was only a sham, someone to barter.
My lover has been my father. Angus has been my lover,
the only man who caused me to feel twined hate and desire
like a rope round my heart. Heal that with your charms
and your herbs. Heal that with your riddles and spells.
Heal the sight that kept you from seeing all these years.
I'll heal my hate with this ax.

BRIGIT: Elen, what kept you from coming to me?

ELEN: Go to you who praised each ugly head he carved?
What would you have done?

BRIGIT: I would have stopped him had I known.

ELEN: He made me promise not to tell.

He kept me silent in his spell.
While you who brewed the remedies for all my childhood ills;
you, who brought me into this world, never asked the reason
why I kept you many nights beside my bed.

BRIGIT: My own need lay too full upon my breast. I should have known his
love for his sweet babe was more than he could bear.

ELEN: How can you defend him even now?

BRIGIT: Not defend him, Elen, only think what life has done.

ELEN: I was your rival for his love those years. I was the one who triumphed
over you.

BRIGIT: You were a child. I was captive of desire and I starved while he grew
satiate and fat off his own child.

ELEN: He told me I was wiser than the wisest woman alive. He told me I was
born with knowledge of the ways of love.

BRIGIT: He lied.

ELEN: He told me I desired each caress; he said my writhing body kept his
hand upon my flesh. I was born to pleasure him, he said.

BRIGIT: He lied. You were a child, born innocent and sweet.

ELEN: You gave me to his grasp. You turned away, and I gave all my love to
him. If I cared how you betrayed my trust I would be sharpening this
ax to move along your throat. But, so help me, Brigit, I do not.

BRIGIT: Elen, listen, if you can. You are blameless; you have always been.

ELEN: Stop! I learned how at my father's knee, and I seduced the king.
I am her murderess. I took her love away as surely as I once took
yours from you.

BRIGIT: Even so, I did not die. I lived. And she will do what she must do. But I
must go to her and bring these herbs. Elen, put the ax down. I have a
simpler revenge. I have herbs in my bag you can mix and put in his
mead. They will bring on a fever that will leave him unmanned. Put

the ax down. Try this potion first. Let him live with time to reflect what he's done. And let you live free of the murderer's curse. You have enough to carry in your heart, and I in mine.

[VINCENT *comes from the house.*]

VINCENT: Where have you been? Etain is awake. She cries in her pains. Come into the house.

BRIGIT: Elen, do as I asked. One part of each of these herbs. Boil, then cool. I am more helpless before Etain's rage than I am before yours. The murder she plans is harder still to undo.

[*She exits with* VINCENT.]

SCENE SIX

[*The dolmen.* MACHA *sits at its base, singing amidst the songs of the birds.*]

MACHA: There go the crows in the sky.
One for sorrow.
Two for joy.
Three for a girl.
Four for a boy.
What will you be,
little bird that lives
in my nest—a creature like myself,
or a man-child, strange and unknown?
A woman of sorrow and comfort and joy,
or a man-child, silent, withdrawn,
frightened, thinking he's strong?
If you're a boy, little lamb, little bird,
humming inside my flesh, if you're a boy,
not one like myself, as known as I am known,
what can I do to help you remain a child
of sorrow and comfort and joy? What can I do,
as you grow to a man, to help you be known to yourself,
to live your mystery through, to give of your warmth,

[139]

your sorrow, your joy to all who would ask it of you?

[OWAIN *and* IAN *approach the mountainside.*]

OWAIN: Did you hear that song?

IAN: I heard nothing, Sire.

OWAIN: Come, man, stop lying.

IAN: O, the song of the crows. Certainly, Sire, I did hear the singing of birds.

OWAIN: And a woman's voice among them.

IAN: That I did not hear. We are but a mile from the barn, where Macha has gone with the lamb. Let us make haste.

OWAIN: There's a woman alone by the dolmen. That is the woman I saw. Is that woman your "wife"?

IAN: My wife went down to the barn. I would seek her there.

OWAIN: Look. What do you see? Describe that woman to me.

IAN: Which woman, Lord? My wife, or that shadow against the rock.

OWAIN: Are they not the same?

MACHA: Must you stand in the midst of the morning sun and disrupt the birds' calls with your quarrel? I am the woman you seek, if you seek after Macha herself.

OWAIN: I have heard a great tale of your strength from this man.

MACHA: I have asked him not to be bragging.

OWAIN: If he lied, he will pay, for he angered me with his words.

MACHA: What could a poor shepherd say to anger someone proud as a king?

OWAIN: He spoke at great length of the beauty and strength of his wife, till it came to my mind that if such a woman lived she ought to be wife of a lord.

MACHA: She ought to be wife of no man, but a creature unto herself.

OWAIN: The shepherd has said his wife could defeat Owain himself.

MACHA [to IAN]: Did you say that?

IAN: I only praised your wondrous ways. You know how I am with words, if one rolls easily off my tongue a thousand and one rush behind it. Oh, I wove a wondrous web. You would have loved how I spoke, for you love to hear yourself praised when we sit by the fire in the glade. Should I die for my glorious words, or the wondrous spell that I wove?

MACHA: You see, he has only imagined my strength. It's natural enough, alone with the sheep, to weave songs and wonderful myths.

OWAIN: I saw you at dawn, racing the sun to the barn. This shepherd you seek to protect has bartered his life for his wife. Wrestle me or he dies for his boast.

MACHA: Gladly, my Lord. I will meet you in one month's time.

OWAIN: You will meet me this day.

MACHA: I am heavy with child. I would not wrestle now.

OWAIN: Then he dies for his brag. Come, man, say goodbye to your wife.

IAN: Macha, please, do as he says. I tremble so hard for my life. A wife should protect her spouse. You are duty bound to wrestle the Lord.

MACHA: Ach, you are a weak and stupid man, after all. Are
all those of your sex who practice a gentle touch
weak in the brain? I am no more beholden to you
than the birds that fly free in the sky must freeze
for the arrow or stone. You bartered your life for a lie.

[To OWAIN.]

I am not this man's wife. Now, go on your way.

[141]

IAN: Macha, please, don't let me die. I did what I did with no thought of harm. I'm an innocent man about to be slain.

MACHA: If you do not sense the evil you do using me as a jewel or coin to purchase your worth over his, I sense not the evil I do letting you die as you should.

OWAIN: If he is not your husband, I claim you as mine. You are an unprotected woman on my land.

MACHA: Your land . . .

OWAIN: Aye, mine, and my father's before me, and my son's to come. All who stop here owe obedience to my line.

MACHA: No more than the rain or the wind, or the glorious moon that snatched your sun the other day. I am not of a race that obeys the owners of land.

OWAIN: Wrestle me and win. I'll grant that the woman who dares such a feat belongs to no one but herself.

MACHA: I have other cares on my mind than proving my strength to a man.

OWAIN: Refuse and I'll drive you far from this place and plant this man's head on a stake in the ground.

MACHA: This is the place to which I've come; this is the place where I belong.

OWAIN: Wrestle and win, I'll grant you the right to remain and do as you wish. Wrestle and lose, I'll make you my queen. Refuse, I'll drive you away.

MACHA: We will meet at noon in the yard in front of the house.
I would wrestle you close to the one who is your wife.
Go, now leave me alone.

[*The men exit.*]

MACHA: I don't suppose you'd care to be born
quite as soon as I'd wish. O, well, little bird, little
lamb, stay where you are. You've taught me as no one

has, we do for life what is asked, with no thought of gain
or control, and life responds as it will. Stay with me,
now, little beast. If I grow frightened or tense, sing
to me with yourself. Startle me with your kicks. Beat
your wings under my heart. Bind me to life. Come, now,
we need to deck ourselves out for the battle we're bound
to win. But why, little one, are these men either
foolish or hard? What is the thrill of their cruel ways?
And why do they fear a woman grown heavy with child?

SCENE SEVEN

[MACHA *girds for the fight. She walks from the dolmen to Angus's workplace, to the yard in front of* OWAIN's *house.*]

MACHA: No matter, my child. What a tale you'll have to tell
when you're old, how before you were born you battled a lord
for the right to belong to yourself. We'll make a beautiful cloak
from feathers left by the birds: black from the raven's back,
red from the cardinal's breast, grey from the swallow's wings,
blue from the throat of the jay, silver brought from the sea
by the gull; woven by threads of lichen and moss
into a wonderful cloak.

[MACHA *stoops and picks up from the ground a cloak of feathers in beautiful bright colors. She puts it on and approaches* ANGUS's *yard. He is at work, carving.*]

MACHA: Carve me the mask of a crow, quickly now.

ANGUS: Ho, who might you be? You're not a human woman at all, I'm
thinking, but a fairy queen come from the hills of the sidhe.

MACHA: Make me the mask as I've asked, quick as you can.

ANGUS [*working to fashion a crow's mask*]: Yes, my lady, right away. It's an honor
to serve the fairy folk. I'm a poor man with an unmarried daughter to
care for but I don't ask for payment from the race of immortals. I
wouldn't take gold if it were offered. Gold's fit payment for grave-

stones, coffins and crosses. But gold for the face of a crow to hide a goddess's brow is no proper payment at all. I'm touched to be asked, truly I am. I think you'll be pleased with my craft. There aren't many around with the skill to perform such a task, but I'm specially trained in the ritual making of masks. I understand, if you'll pardon my frankness, how without a mask, even a goddess . . . People need to be shown what to believe. This is a visual age. When I was a boy a story would do just as well. But no more. Now it's the splendid effects that stir up the hearts of the crowd.

[*He holds the mask up to her face, then resumes work on it.*]

I hope you'll remember me well to the race that dwells under the hill, beyond the wave, in all hidden corners of the world. It isn't payment I ask, but I wonder if a cup of their magic wine might be left on my threshold some night? The kind that keeps them eternally young. Barely enough to quench a slight thirst is all that I ask. Just enough to bring back my youth.

[*He fits the mask to her face.*]

There you are. The glorious mask of a crow. The bird that knows more than we know. Whoever looks straight into the eyes of a crow is bewitched on the spot. A fine piece of work, if I say so myself. Don't thank me, now. I've skills to share with the fairy folk. Perhaps you'll remember my words. If they could spare a cup of that drink, I'd delight in the thought that my flesh might remain as alive and alert as the spirit I put in my work.

[MACHA *vanishes;* ANGUS *leaps with joy.*] It's done. One glass of fairy wine, I will be young. Young enough to beat young Owain at his games. I'll challenge him and I will win. The hunt, the crown, the women he takes to bed will all be mine.

ELEN [*carrying a cup full of drink*]: Father, who are you talking to?

ANGUS: A woman come from the sidhe. I asked for a cup of their wine, the kind that keeps them eternally young, if you know what I mean. I carved her a wonderful mask. I took no payment at all.

ELEN [*offering him the cup*]: It's no fairy drink, but it has a healing effect. It's passable good, with a strong effect on the glands.

ANGUS: You are a good girl, Elen, aren't you now. You do care about your father after all.

[*He takes a long, deep drink.*]

SCENE EIGHT

[MACHA *approaches the yard. As she comes, everyone comes.* OWAIN, IAN, ELEN, ANGUS, VINCENT, *the* CROW-WOMEN *gather, waiting for her. Only* BRIGIT *and* ETAIN *are not present.*]

VINCENT: Your wife is in labor inside.

OWAIN: I will be with her soon.
I have business with one who comes from the mountain beyond,
who taunts and who chides with her strength—
who, I have heard, caused Etain to grow weak.

[MACHA *appears, in cloak and mask, her body oiled, her breasts exposed, her belly big. She stands, ready to fight, in front of* OWAIN.]

You come like a goddess to me.

MACHA: As you have dreamed me, I have come.
As you have feared, I am.

OWAIN [*stripping*]: Now the fight begins
between desire and will.

MACHA: Now the fight must start
between the conquered and the unconquered heart.

[*They begin to circle one another, as wrestlers.*]

OWAIN: You are the earth and I, the sky.
Under my light you grow fertile and rich.

MACHA: I am the sea that holds all life in its womb.
You are the restless need to be born and to die.

[145]

OWAIN: You are what was when the world began.
I am the life of the people, the life of the tribe.

MACHA: I am the force inside the rock, the wave,
the flight of the bird.

OWAIN: I am the striving heart, casting desire out of itself.

MACHA: I am the force you can neither grasp nor escape.

OWAIN: I am the need for a glory not of this world.

MACHA: I am only what is, despised and disfigured by need.

OWAIN: I am man in battle with fear.

MACHA: I am life, the thing feared.

OWAIN: You are the one who taunts, who goads.

MACHA: You are the taunted, wounded by loss.

OWAIN: This is the fight that has always been.

MACHA: Between the birther and the one born.

OWAIN: This the struggle that has no end.

> [*They begin the wrestling match. It is done in silence and continues for a long time. The two shining bodies, one lithe, one large with child, lock and entwine in all manner of positions. Their fight is half sexual, half brutal. It is in deadly earnest and has about it a fierce, elemental beauty. The fight finally ceases when* OWAIN *is pinned to the ground. In this position, he seems* MACHA's *child at last. From the house there is a loud, anguished cry.* BRIGIT *appears, and the focus shifts to her; she carries the newborn son.*]

BRIGIT: Your fight is senseless, ageless, without end. A woman has just died. And all of you who mocked her, who held yourselves apart or different from her—you, too, are dead inside, are deadened by the terrible death she died, died in pain upon her birthing bed. I gave her herbs to drink. I caressed the lips that parted to expose the child's head. I chanted and placed straw beneath her bed. None of the old ways worked. She sought out pain and death as if pain and death alone spoke in words she understood. "I've sinned," she screamed. "I have been wild, animal-like. I've sinned or I would not suffer so." I rubbed her flesh with oil. She stiffened underneath my hand. "The punishment for sin is death," she cried. "There is no sin," I said. She pushed my head away. "You lie." I saw the corpse give up the child. The woman dead delivered him safely from her gravid womb.

[THE PEOPLE *set up a keening wail. They go to claim the body of* ETAIN, *leaving* MACHA *and* OWAIN.]

MACHA: My labor has begun.
    I leave you as you left Etain.
    But as victor in the fight she lost
    I have power to curse you, power I will use.
    From this day on you will be changed
    as any woman-girl who changes to the mother she has sought.
    Each time you try to prove your strength
    you will be as overcome as any woman giving birth.
    You have lost the power to fight in this fight you lost.
    Men will mock you and betray you, defeat you, blame you.
    You will be as helpless as Etain, as chained as she was
    chained to life. You will grow humble in the service
    of the force that only uses you to manifest itself.

SCENE NINE

[MACHA *has gone to the sea to have her child. The procession approaches the dolmen, bearing the body of* ETAIN. *They lay her in the earth, but as they try to bury her, the earth rejects the body of the woman dead too soon. The earth heaves up the shape of a woman's body from beneath itself. It refuses to cover* ETAIN. *It is as if the earth labors to birth the dead* ETAIN. *And, in fact, an old Celtic legend says that the earth will refuse the body of someone dead before his time. The people here witness the proof of that legend, and they chant their responses to the awesome event.*]

WOMEN'S VOICES: Etain, we bid you go beneath the earth
    to enter once again upon the course
    of life eternal, life renewing life.

MEN'S VOICES [*as the corpse is thrown up*]:
    The earth won't take the body back.
    The earth spits up the corpse.

FIOLA: Where is my home, the homeless body cries,
    if not within the earth's moist breast?
    Where is my rest, the tortured self demands,
    if not within the one from which I came?

VINCENT: Mary, Mother of God, pray for us now
    in our hour of need. Etain has died for her sins.

WOMEN'S VOICES: Etain, we give you gently to the earth.
    The earth will wrap her flesh around your own.

VINCENT: The penalty for sin is death. Did she sin
    against herself? Mother of God, forgive.

[ETAIN's *body is thrown violently up from the earth.*]

MEN'S VOICES: The corpse is laid within the earth;
    again, the earth throws back the body of Etain.

DIEDRE: Where is delight for me, where peace,
    if not within the center of the earth?

WOMEN'S VOICES: Take her back to that most hallowed place,
    the darkest place, the sheltered place,
    the start. There let her be of death until
    she decomposes into life.

VINCENT: The flesh demands our death, the putrid flesh
    must die. The pure, eternal soul lives.

CLEEVNA: Take me back into yourself, my mother lost.
    Let me take root within your moist and sheltered loins.
    Let me become your child again, breathing as you breath,
    alive within the darkness of your womb.

[*Again, the body is heaved up from its place of burial.*]

MEN'S VOICES: The earth throws back Etain into our sight.

[148]

We see the fury of the mother once defied.

WOMEN'S VOICES: The earth is raging in her grief, vengeful,
   violent in her hate of needless death.
   She trembles underneath us like a scourge.
   Mother, we are humbled by your rage.

VINCENT: God in heaven, snatch her soul away from
   all that is corrupt, the heaving earth,
   the stinking flesh. Redeem the purity in us.

MEENA: Oh, let me be at peace, at rest.
   What cause have I to fear? I seek the wetness of
   your flesh, your hot, sweet smells, the shadow
   of your loins. Mother, take me home.

[*The men lay the corpse into the earth again. The earth receives the body of* ETAIN.
MACHA *appears with her child in her arms. She comes from the sea where she has given
birth. She wears a shimmering silver green gown, translucent over her naked frame.
Her hair is long around her shoulders and it glitters with creatures of the sea. She seems
taller. She carries her newborn close to her breast. There is silence.*]

MACHA: Here is a creature washed from the sea.
   She came to me singing her name: Etain,
   Etain. Her song echoed long in my ear;
   she came to me singing her name,
   like tide pounding hard at the shore.
   Etain, Etain. She wore down my wish
   to keep her inside. She tore at my flesh,
   ripped me in two. I am Etain come again,
   she cried. I opened myself to her call.
   There is no love like the love I bear for Etain.
   I bore her out of myself. All that I am, she is.
   I am the sea, Etain the wave. I am the ground,
   she is the hill; I am the sky, she is the sun, the moon.
   All that has form, she is. I am all that is formless,
   senseless, wild, all that is feared or desired.
   She is the hill, the wave, the light.
   She is the mark of my strength.
   She is the proof of my love.

[*Silence. The light shifts. It is day once more.*]

[149]

ACT II

SCENE TEN

[*Twelve years later. Beltane Night, the feast of the spring. Throughout Act II, the flames of a large bonfire are silhouetted in the distance. Dead branches and trees are being burned to herald the new life of the spring. The Beltane fire is also jumped over by those wishing to take into their flesh the power released by the flames. All through the act, the music and singing of the dancers and feasters is heard. Act II opens at the dolmen, halfway down the mountainside from the revels.* BROTHER VINCENT *is chasing a young boy,* CONOR, OWAIN's *son, around the dolmen, trying to catch him. His pants have fallen down around his knees, and he is having trouble escaping the monk.*]

CONOR: Damn these pants. Damn them.

[*He hops behind the dolmen.*]

VINCENT: Add blasphemy to carnal sin. You'll be saying the acts of contrition for days.

CONOR [*from behind the dolmen*]: Please, Brother Vincent, go away. I'll come to you. I promise I will.

VINCENT: I'll come to you since you're easy to catch.

[*He dashes behind the dolmen. Struggling to get his pants up,* CONOR *skitters out through the dolmen. He turns and thumbs his nose at the monk.*]

CONOR: Naaa! Naaa!

VINCENT: Now, where did you go, child with the devil in you?

[*He sees* CONOR, *who begins to hop and run away behind the dolmen but who trips on his pants and falls.*]

VINCENT: Pride goeth before the fall. The good Lord has hobbled you tight as a horse.

[VINCENT *pulls* CONOR *up.*]

CONOR: Damn these pants. Damn them! If I was still in my shirt I'd never have been caught.

VINCENT: Better to damn the hands that were roaming around than damn the man's dress that makes sinning hard.

CONOR: You wear a gown easy to lift up and down!

VINCENT: I am in control of myself.
    You are a victim of lust
    so the good Lord has clothed you in pants.

[VINCENT *pulls* CONOR *down to his knees.*]

Together, my son, let us pray.

[VINCENT *and* CONOR *recite the prayer together, the monk in full voice,* CONOR *weakly and reluctantly.*]

VINCENT and CONOR: "We seek refuge under the protection of your mercies, O Mother of God; do not reject our supplication in need but save us from perdition, oh you who alone are blessed."

VINCENT: Louder, lad. The devil's the only one in earshot of a mumbled prayer.

[*They recite again,* CONOR *yelling.*]

VINCENT and CONOR: "We seek refuge under the protection of your mercies, O Mother of God; do not reject our supplication in need but save us from perdition, oh you who alone are blessed."

VINCENT: Since you've suddenly come into full voice, you can recite alone, fifty times. When you are hoarse, we will know the blessed virgin has heard and has responded with blessed quietude.

CONOR: Fifty times! No. Please! My knees will rot from the damp. I'll take root, I'll sprout.

VINCENT: Begin.

CONOR: Please. Twenty times. I know I've sinned.

VINCENT: Are you fully aware of what you've done?

CONOR: "I seek refuge under the protection of your mercies, O Mother of God; do not reject our supplication in need but save us from perdition, O you who alone are blessed." Nineteen.

VINCENT: Forty-nine! Do you know where I found you committing your sin? Not two steps away from where, twelve years ago, on the day you were born, your mother's soul was committed to God. Not two steps from where she rests, you lay on your back, spewing your seed upon the earth, dreaming, the good Lord knows of what! Why, Conor, why did you pick this spot to do the hideous thing that you did?

CONOR: Everyone's up in the hills having fun but I've been forbidden to go. I wanted to hear the music they make.

VINCENT: So you sprawled across your mother's grave and committed a carnal sin!

CONOR: I lay down and my mind drifted off.

VINCENT: Bewitched, that's what you've been.
Bewitched by that woman up in the hills.
She left us alone for twelve good years.
She comes back, igniting that awful fertility rite,
working her evil against Etain's son!
You are in mortal danger, Conor.

[OWAIN *enters*.]

OWAIN: I won't have you filling the boy's head with lies.

CONOR [*running to his father. Without meaning to,* OWAIN *pulls away*]: Father, please, please, let me go, please let me go up to the hills where the fires burn. Don't they look wonderful grand? Please, father, please.

OWAIN: No, Conor, not this year.

CONOR: Everyone's there. Angus and Ian, Elen, everyone, playing their harps and their pipes. Brigit's there, too, father, please.

OWAIN: I'm not there, neither are you.

CONOR: I didn't mean to sin, father, truly not. If you let me go, I won't sin again, father, I promise I won't.

VINCENT: Conor, go back to the house. We'll finish your prayers in your room.

[CONOR *falls upon his knees and begins to race through two more prayers to the Blessed Virgin.*]

OWAIN: Conor, stop mumbling those words. What have you done? Answer me, lad.

CONOR: Please, father, please. Just let me finish these prayers. I've only to say them forty-seven more times.

OWAIN: What have you done, lad?

VINCENT: The boy has been bewitched . . .

OWAIN: Quiet, let him tell me himself. Conor!

CONOR: I've been very bad.

OWAIN: What have you done? I will have an answer when I ask.

CONOR: I did try to stop myself, truly I did. You know how it is when your mind drifts away; you hear music on the wind.

VINCENT: The boy has been bewitched by the same woman who bewitched Etain. She comes back and look: he has spilled his seed on his mother's grave. He has defiled the spot where she lies.

OWAIN: Quiet. I asked for an answer from my son.

CONOR: I'm sorry, father. I'll never do it again. Only don't say I've been bewitched. I don't want my body to rot.

OWAIN: Get up, lad, get up. So you touch yourself, do you? Before going to bed? [CONOR *nods.*] Hah! At other times, too?

[153]

CONOR: Father, please.

OWAIN: Answer me! In the middle of the day? [OWAIN *laughs*.] At prayers?

CONOR: Father . . .

OWAIN: Answer me, boy.

CONOR: Sometimes, yes . . . but . . .

OWAIN: Does it feel good? [CONOR *is silent*.] Does it feel good, I say! Answer with words.

CONOR: Yes, father.

OWAIN: "Yes, father" what?

CONOR: Yes, father it feels . . . all right.

OWAIN: Hah! You call that bewitched. The boy does what makes him feel good. There's nothing magic in that.

VINCENT: It's the spot. The spot. Who lured him here, with music and songs, to sully his mother's grave?

OWAIN: What happens to boys who do what you've done? Answer me!

CONOR: They go to hell when they die; the worms eat their flesh. They stink with lust.

OWAIN: They grow up to be strong men. They grow up to sire sons. What stinks around here are the lies of the monk. [CONOR *laughs, despite himself*.] Go, Conor, go home to bed. We have a new colt to break in the morning.

[CONOR *goes*.]

What shame are you pumping into my son? Accusing him of what you wished you were man enough to have done. Sin! Nobody here knew what sin was until you came.

VINCENT: I'm raising your son as his mother would have wished. In her faith.

OWAIN: The faith she died from. I should have sent him up to the hills; he would learn to love the flesh for the pleasure it brings. If Etain had known that she might still be alive.

VINCENT: Look at those flames, eating the earth, licking away at the sky. Hellfire is loose in those hills. Of course, you kept him away. You sense the evil the wild woman brings.

OWAIN: It's not evil I sense.

VINCENT: Have you forgotten the struggle we had to bury Etain in this ground? You know the wild woman up in the hills and the midwife with her potions and spells took the life from Etain.

OWAIN: If Etain had wanted to live, she would have; I'm not freeing myself from the blame, but I'll not be blaming blameless women.

VINCENT: Then why aren't you dancing with them? Why did Etain's death make you chaste when her life couldn't?

OWAIN: I've learned how to savor desire, perhaps; or, perhaps, it's loss I love most.

VINCENT: Have you thought how loss empties the soul so that faith might fill it? Owain, I would build a church on this spot.

OWAIN: This is a burial mound. It is a sacred spot. Build your church somewhere else.

VINCENT: The people have worshipped here since time began. It would seem natural to them to add God to their pagan tribe. Slowly, they'll learn the truth of the one true Lord. I want to build a church to Etain's memory, consecrated to the blessed Virgin Mary.

OWAIN: Not on this spot. No. Not on my land.

VINCENT: Your land has to be cleansed. As long as the memory remains of Etain's body being heaved up from the earth, Brigit and that wild woman from the hills will hold sway over the people's hearts.

OWAIN: I belong to the old ways.

VINCENT: Then why don't you practice them?

OWAIN: I practice as well as I can.

VINCENT: The new faith doesn't intend to destroy the old. The old faith is
floundering by itself. The new faith is vital and young, a faith of bold
fathers and sons. People need to be forgiven, Owain, for what they've
done. The Church offers that: forgiveness from sin. Who among us
does not need to know we are forgiven some terrible wrong? Who
among us does not need to forget and learn to believe in a merciful
redeeming love? Etain loved this land, in sight of the hills and the sea.
She'd be living now if a church had been built when she came as your
bride. A church would have kept this land free of the spell the wild
woman wove. A church will do so yet. Owain, you might return to
yourself.

OWAIN: I am closer to myself than I have ever been,
though I lack the action to show it.

VINCENT: Build a church. Manifest what you've become.

OWAIN: Enough! I have heard you through.
For the rest of the night, I want to hear music
coming down from the hills.

SCENE ELEVEN

[IAN and ELEN enter. They have come from the Beltane feast. IAN pulls ELEN by the
hand.]

IAN: Here, right here is the spot
where I should have fought.
I ought to have murdered that man,
Lord though he be, when he sought my wife.
All would be changed if I'd done as I should—
chopped off his head, ripped out his heart.
I would be king of the Beltane feast,
the women would flock around me.

[156]

But . . . what good is remorse? If I had it to do
over again, you can be sure I'd do what I said.
If someone comes bothering you, you come to me!
I'd knock the man down, trample him into the ground.

ELEN: Leave me alone.

IAN: What?

ELEN: Leave me alone.

IAN: I thought we came here to . . . well . . . you asked me to come. It's
Beltane night, we ought to . . . it's the right thing to do. It encourages
growth of the crops and easy birth of the lambs.

ELEN: I am sick of the feast and my father's songs.

IAN: Elen, I'm not the man I once was. Don't make me pay for the past. I
was weak and pliable then, but I tell you, it's true, it's my own life I'd
give defending you.

ELEN: Leave me alone.

IAN: How can I leave such beauty alone?

ELEN: Get out of my sight or I'll knock you down the mountainside, till
you end up in the barn caught in the arms of one of your lambs.

IAN [backing away]: All right, all right, I'm off. I can't stand a rage, really, I
can't. I'm sorry, I thought . . . well, no harm was done . . . I'll go back to
my flocks and my dreams. I'll leave you alone with your hate.

[IAN goes. VINCENT approaches ELEN; he has overheard the exchange.]

VINCENT: He's right, for once. Here you are alone with your hate, and the
pain on your face.

ELEN: What do you want?

VINCENT: I was kneeling at Etain's grave, thanking the Lord for the peace
He has given her. I heard what was said.

[157]

ELEN: Better give peace to those still alive than to the dead.

VINCENT: That, too, He can do. What is it, Elen, puts you into such pain?

ELEN: Did you love Etain? Do you hate me because I ran with her man?

VINCENT: God will forgive what you did, if you open your heart. Come, Elen, speak, unburden yourself.

ELEN: Go back to your prayers.

VINCENT: If you speak from your heart, understanding will come. That is God's grace.

ELEN: There are things in this world from which even your god turns his head.

VINCENT: Elen, I have stood where you stand. My flesh has been pulled toward a spot my spirit disowned. I coveted another man's wife. I have fallen asleep in boys' arms. For years, I lived in hot longing and pain. Do you know what I am saying? No act has been more forbidden than one act I once lived for. I was drawn by my need toward my God. Do you think the Lord God, my Father, whom I invoke on my knees does not forgive?

ELEN: Hush. Do you hear that full voice singing songs up the hill? That is my father. Do you hear? I would go to him now, sit at his feet, let him run his hand through my hair. I would be lost in the spell he weaves till I woke and all that remained of his touch was my hate of the foul desire I had felt. Does your god shudder when he hears that?

VINCENT: Do you think God would turn from your pain when He embraced me in mine? Come, we will seek out our Lord. You will lose yourself in his love. He is the Father your soul desires. He will fill your heart with His love.

SCENE TWELVE

[CONOR *has sneaked up the hill to the Beltane rites and the Beltane fire. He meets* ETAIN, MACHA's *daughter, on the edge of the festival grounds, gathering sticks to be burnt in the flames. Silhouetted behind them a large fire burns.*]

CONOR: Hello.

ETAIN: Hello.

CONOR: What are you doing?

ETAIN: Gathering dead branches and roots
to be burned in the Beltane flames.

CONOR: What for?

ETAIN: The fire will free from bough and from branch
the spirit death trapped in death's shape.

CONOR: I don't understand.

ETAIN: On Beltane we leap over the flames,
we take the fire into our veins.
Everything frozen and dead kindles
the life of the spring.

CONOR: How odd.

ETAIN: Odd? I thought everyone knew of Beltane.
Where are you from?

CONOR: I live in the big house below. And you?

ETAIN: I live in the hills or in caves close to the sea.
I live where I want to be.
Come, do you want to leap over the fire?

CONOR: I can't go any closer.

ETAIN: Then leap over me. [*She rolls on the earth.*]

I am your Beltane flame.
I am the fire loose in your veins.

[CONOR *jumps over her, then rolls on the ground.*]

CONOR: Leap over me.
I am fire. I am flame.

[ETAIN *leaps over him.*]

ETAIN: Ouch. You're hot.

CONOR: I'm next, I'm next.

[ETAIN *squats; he leaps over her back.*]

You burn, you burn.

[*He turns and leaps back.*]

You're wild with heat, Beltane flame.

ETAIN [*rising and taking* CONOR's *hands*]: You can sing this song as you leap:
Bless me and all living things I love.
All kine and crops, all flocks and grain,
Bless the spirit that is inside
each tree, each well, each rock.
Bless each shape-change from fish to fowl to fox.
Bless me and all living things I love.

CONOR [*looking at her hard*]: What else do you do on Beltane?

ETAIN: Whatever you wish.

CONOR: What if you're caught?

ETAIN: Caught?

CONOR: What if you do something wrong and someone older finds out?

ETAIN: What could you do wrong on Beltane?

[*She begins to sing the Beltane blessing. The two children join hands and dance.*]

Bless me and all living things I love,

[160]

all kine and crops, all flocks and grain,
nuts and seeds, day and night,
from Hallow Eve to Beltane Eve,
Bless me and all living things I love.

[ANGUS *appears. He walks with the aid of an elaborately gnarled stick.*]

ANGUS: You could sneak away from your house, against your father's will, eh, Conor?

CONOR [*with a start*]: Angus, you wouldn't tell?

ANGUS: We'll see; what will you do for me?

CONOR: I'll see my father raises your rents if you tell. I'll not be threatened by you.

ANGUS: Go along home, boy. You don't belong here. It's the duty of your father's folk not to keep secrets from him.

CONOR [*to* ETAIN]: Tell me your name.

ETAIN: Etain.

CONOR: That was my mother's name.

ANGUS: Go along home.

CONOR: Etain, when can I see you again?

ETAIN: Wherever you find me, there I'll be.
In cave or tree, wind or sea.

ANGUS: Go on, Conor, go. You're over your head.
Go back to your house and your bed.

CONOR [*goes, but as he does he sings to* ETAIN]:
Bless me and all living things I love.
Etain, her hair, her eyes, her voice, her dance . . .

ETAIN: Why did you drive him away?
Everyone is welcome on Beltane Night.

ANGUS: He is not of our faith.

ETAIN: Nonsense. So what?

ANGUS: The church would destroy Beltane Night.

ETAIN: Why would it want to do that?

ANGUS: The church wants one god.

ETAIN: It should have whatever it wants. One
    more god would be fine.

ANGUS [*laughing*]: You are a wonderful child. You're not like your mother.
    You're soft like the other Etain.

ETAIN: Since we've been camped in these hills
    I have felt called by a voice,
    a voice so lovely and sad I would go wherever it called
    and do whatever it bid.
    Do you think it could be Etain?

ANGUS: She died the day you were born.
    Some say your mother cast the spell that killed her.

ETAIN: My mother's never done harm.

ANGUS: I did some work for her once.
    I asked for some small thing in return.
    From that day to this, I've walked with a cane.

ETAIN: Stop lying, old man.

ANGUS: She crippled me for no cause. But, tonight, child,
    for the first time, I feel the old juices running again.
    I need you, Etain, to take off your mother's spell.
    Come here, little girl, little swallow, little gull.

ETAIN: You're scaring me.

ANGUS: You have beautiful breasts, like the buds of springtime themselves.
    Come, sit on my knee. Let me touch those little buds.

ETAIN: Stop.

ANGUS: We won't tell your mother a thing.
    You'll make me well but we won't tell her how.
    Etain, you're beautiful, pure.
    You're like my own child to me.

    [ANGUS *kisses her.* ETAIN *strikes him.* MACHA *and* BRIGIT *enter. The* CROWS *appear too, flapping angrily around* ANGUS.]

MACHA: Leave my daughter alone.

    [ETAIN *runs to* MACHA.]

    Get off this mountain.
    You soil Beltane.

BRIGIT: Once you used your own daughter while I shut my eyes.
    Now I see. Go from this mountain. Get away from me.

    [*The* CROWS *cry out again.*]

ANGUS: Without me, the faith dies.

MACHA: The faith has no place for a man
    who does not know deception from love,
    who puts his needs before the needs of the young,
    who uses life for himself.

BRIGIT [*rousing the* CROWS, *which go after* ANGUS]:
    Cast him out of the faith.
    Banish him from our sight.
    Let him go comfortless, evermore.

    [*The* CROWS *chase* ANGUS *off the mountainside.* BRIGIT *sinks down under her cloak; she becomes part of the mountain, a rock.*]

ETAIN: He's a creepy, cruddy, curdly dog;
    a mangy, mucky, squishy frog.
    Let's put him in our brew and cook him up!

MACHA: Let's burn him out of our minds,
    banish him from our dreams.

[CONOR *has stolen up the hill from the other side.*]

CONOR: Etain . . .

ETAIN [*running to him*]: You should never have left me alone with that horrible old man.

CONOR: Etain, I had to see you again.

MACHA: Who are you, lad?

CONOR: Lord Conor, Lord Owain's son.

MACHA: Etain's child.

CONOR: My mother is dead.

MACHA: You carry her eyes and her pride.

CONOR: Who are you?

MACHA: Macha, Etain's mother, and your mother's friend.
I knew her before you were born.

CONOR: Oh.

MACHA: Why so sad?

CONOR: It's my fault she died.

MACHA: Who tells you that?

CONOR: I read it in everyone's eyes.

MACHA: You are her child. She, too, read through to the heart with a gaze.

ETAIN: Oh, Conor, it's not true. You didn't kill your mother.
Come, Conor, catch me. I have so much to tell you.

[*As the children run off*, OWAIN *appears.*]

OWAIN: Conor! You will be punished for this.

CONOR: You can whip me tomorrow!

MACHA: Stalking your son?

OWAIN: Is that what you think?

MACHA: That's what I see.

OWAIN: For twelve years I've lived
   with the taste of your sweat on my tongue.

MACHA: Etain's son is a fine lad.

OWAIN: Why are you here?

MACHA: I left my dead on this land.
   I birthed on this shore.

OWAIN: Is that all?

MACHA: I was called to the Beltane rite.

OWAIN: I have wanted you.

MACHA: You've come.

OWAIN: Yes.

MACHA: The conquered come back.

OWAIN: And those who aren't conquered yet.

MACHA: There is no one like that.

OWAIN: No one not conquered by you?

MACHA: By whatever has knotted the heart.

OWAIN: It was done with your arms round my back.

MACHA: It was done long before I appeared.
   I am not your way out.

OWAIN: You are the future I want.

MACHA: We are driven by something else.

OWAIN: By desire itself.

MACHA: By all that we've lost.

OWAIN: Twelve years you've roamed . . . a woman alone.

MACHA: Cast out. Lied about.

OWAIN: Afraid to take what you've won.

MACHA: My freedom was what I fought for.
    Do you come offering that?

OWAIN: I offer you freedom from self.

MACHA: Where will I be?

OWAIN: Spirit to naked spirit with me.

MACHA: Faceless and lost.

OWAIN: Fleshless through flesh and found.

MACHA: What will I learn?

OWAIN: How flame speaks to flame.
    How white light rises from the earth's bowels.
    How music is made.

MACHA: Why must I know?

OWAIN: Because we are one and the same
    slipped through the other's flesh
    painless and safe into life.

MACHA: Those are wonderful words that you speak.
    I was last wooed by words in a shepherd's hut.

OWAIN: I offer you the house of a king.

MACHA: He bade me fight for my life.

OWAIN: I offer you a king's strength.

MACHA: Such strength means a fight in the yard,
    more fights if I follow you back.

OWAIN: I offer you a king's love.

MACHA: No, Owain, it is not right.

OWAIN: When? I will wait.

MACHA: In another world, perhaps. In a next life.

OWAIN: Don't play with me.
    I want you as my queen, now, in this life.
    Tonight.

MACHA: I am not meant for the part.
    Etain was well cast.

OWAIN: Etain is twelve years dead.

MACHA: Etain lives in my heart.

OWAIN: And in mine. But I cannot live in the past.
    I cannot live without love. And you, will you
    live cold and alone day and night?

MACHA: I do not.

OWAIN: There is someone else?

MACHA: There is all this,
    a world that I love,
    a child, and, above all else,
    I go in service
    to what is unlived,
    to all that we might become.

It is a fierce, terrible love.

OWAIN: I can share that.

MACHA: Perhaps, in your time, in your way.

[MACHA *turns and begins to leave; the two stand apart as the children come running in.*]

ETAIN: This is how Macha did it. She wrestled him right to the ground!

[*They roll around.*]

CONOR: Stop, Etain, stop.
Let's be our mothers, the lambs—wild and free.
I want to be like my mother was when she lived.

ETAIN: Catch me, if you can. I am my mother, the ewe. You are yours.

[*They scamper about.*]

CONOR: O, I am heavy with lamb. Quick, Etain, rub my belly.

ETAIN [*sings*]: Poor, fat ewe, you are big with the lamb you must birth.
Throw back your head and laugh in the wind.
Throw back your head because effort is love
and death must lose in the end.

CONOR: Baaa! Baaa!
Is that what my mother did?

ETAIN: She did.

CONOR: Brother Vincent would call that sin.

ETAIN: What is sin?

CONOR: Something that feels good.

ETAIN: Let me try. [*She lets out a long animal bray, like a scream of love.*]
Baaa! Baaa!

Rub my belly, Conor, rub my belly now.

[CONOR *comes to rub her belly and they fall, tumbling and laughing on the ground together. They tumble around, until, suddenly, they fall into a deep child's sleep on the ground, their bodies curved in an S-shape, one against the other, their arms intertwined in a manner that seems to make the two into one. Silence. The Beltane fire burns.* BRIGIT *rises and covers the children with her cloak.*]

BRIGIT: Here is one boy and one girl to bless as the Beltane night ends.

[*She sinks down. The* CROWS *hover around her.*]

MACHA [*to* OWAIN]: There is the next life of which I spoke.

OWAIN: They are children at play.
    What do they know of loss or of love?

MACHA: Learn the deep reaches of your son.

OWAIN: I will learn whatever you wish; come home with me.

MACHA: Beltane is over and done.
    I will be gone.

OWAIN: You are needed here.
    Come with me, as my queen.

MACHA: Go.
    Let me be.
    Go home with your son.

OWAIN [*turning his disappointment into anger at his son*]:
    Get up.
    You have disobeyed and been caught.
    You came here against my will and saw things I had forbidden to you.
    Get down the hill to your bed. Wipe the thought of this night
    from your eyes. There's a colt to be broken at dawn,
    wild birds to be hunted and slain. I want you manly and brave
    in the morn.

[*He takes* CONOR *roughly by the shoulder and pushes him down the hill.*]

[169]

MACHA: Paah! He knows nothing yet.

BRIGIT [*rising and going toward* MACHA]:
    Perhaps not, but I have thought things out.
    I, too, waited twelve years,
    looking about, searching my heart. This year
    I called you to me.

MACHA: You have been with me since the sun set.
    Midwife, we have birthed this night,
    and will wash ourselves fresh in the dawn.
    Yet I don't know why I was called to this spot.

BRIGIT: I am old.
    The autumn tree seeks full color and form.
    Had I knelt with you by the sea
    that night many years ago
    and coaxed the child from you to me,
    my longing might have been over and done.
    Had I shared your struggle and known your eyes
    wild with effort and love, my heart might have drunk
    its full from your writhing and cries.

MACHA: Yet you did none of those things
    and left me alone until Beltane.

BRIGIT: Tonight the past found its full shape
    and slipped far back in my heart. All of the past,
    that is, except one missed sea birth.
    Were I not old I might forget
    in the passions of years to come
    so simple a trust that never had been.
    But age cannot silence the torturous scream
    for what is perfect and gone.
    Age is the ageless keen,
    keening the greed of love.

MACHA: Why am I not afraid when you speak of greed?

BRIGIT: I am offering self to you.

MACHA: You will leave your home?

BRIGIT: I will teach you and Etain my herbs.
My healing lore is my home; I carry that where I go.

MACHA: You will bond your strength to ours?

BRIGIT: If we had been bonded since time began,
much we have sought would have come.

MACHA: Let us bathe by the light of the dawn.

[*They go to the spring which has bubbled up on the spot. They begin to bathe one another gently.*]

BRIGIT: The spring wells up once a year from the earth's core.

MACHA: What tales does it tell?

BRIGIT: Lost souls seeking return play on their pipes
at the river's source.
They send their longing to us.

[ETAIN *wakes.*]

ETAIN: Mother . . . where have you gone?

MACHA: Here I am, child, here.

BRIGIT: It is dawn.

MACHA: Come, wash yourself in the spring.

ETAIN: I don't want to wash myself clean.
Beltane was a wonderful dream.
Only one stain, that old man, can be washed out.
Let the rest be.

BRIGIT: You're filthy, child.

ETAIN: Yes, I smell of the flock and the barn.
I smell like the ewe. Let me be.
It's a wonderful smell to me.

[171]

MACHA: All right, wild one, you can stay.
   Just let me touch your lips with water
   from deep in the earth. Take a drink.
   You don't even need to wash your face.

ACT III

SCENE THIRTEEN

[*The same scene, a morning after Beltane.* ETAIN *is older now, perhaps sixteen.
Time and no time at all has passed. The* CROWS *dance around* ETAIN, *waking her from
her dream.*]

CROWS: Wake, Etain, wake.
   You are grown.
   You are no longer a child
   asleep on a hill,
   dreaming of things you could not know.
   Wake as a woman wakes
   smiling of night,
   desire awake in her heart.

ETAIN: Mother . . . where have you gone?

CROWS: Gone off with Brigit.

ETAIN: The birds sang. Gone off with Brigit?

CROWS: The girl's heart cried.

ETAIN: Where have you gone?

CROWS: Far from this place, locked in her arms.

ETAIN: Gone from me, gone?

CROWS: Flown away, as if they were one.

ETAIN: Flown away, flown, the birds' song sang.

CROWS: Gone from me, gone, the girl's heart cried.

ETAIN: Gone, mother, gone?

CROWS: Gone. Gone. Gone from Etain. Gone away.

ETAIN: Gone with Brigit?

CROWS: The girl's heart cried.

ETAIN: Why, mother, why?
    I am here.

CROWS: Why, mother, why,
    the girl's heart cried.

ETAIN: To find what I never had,
    the mocking crows said.

CROWS: To find what I never had.

[*The* CROWS *begin to change into their garments as peasant women, taking off crow-masks and wings, putting on their heavy, dull work clothes.*]

ETAIN: But I had a wonderful dream.

CLEEVNA: A dream, the girl said.

ETAIN: I dreamt of a bird flying free
    and the sound of the wave on the shore.

MEENA: The girl's heart leapt.

ETAIN: I am grown.

FIOLA: Grown, mother, grown,
    the girl's heart sang.

ETAIN: Grown and alone. I am free.

DIEDRE: I am free.
  The girl's heart stopped.

CLEEVNA: We must go, too.

ETAIN: Where, where must you go?

DIEDRE: Down the hill to the house.

CLEEVNA: The house that sits by the shore.

FIOLA: We must spin the wool from
  the just-sheared sheep.

ETAIN: I will go, too.

MEENA: No. No. You must stay here on the hill.

ETAIN: No, I will go. I will help with your work.

MEENA: No, Etain, no. The work turns us ugly and old.

DIEDRE: The work makes us tired and dull.

CLEEVNA: The work is done for someone else.

FIOLA: You must stay far from the house.

ETAIN: I will disguise myself.

  [*She picks up a rag from the ground, one of the* CROWS' *cloaks, to put over the shimmering gown that she wears.*]

  I will come help with your work.
  When it is through, I will run down to the sea.

ALL: No, Etain, no.

ETAIN: Look, look at that bird
  flying down to the shore,
  a heron, silver and free.
  Don't you hear that bird
  calling to me?

[174]

[*She runs off.*]

DIEDRE: After her, quick.
　　She is gone.

FIOLA: She flees the life of the mountain tops.

MEENA: To run down to the sea
　　where she was born.

ALL: To be born to desire again.

MEENA: After her, quick.

ALL: Women like us, bent and slow
　　from our work, are helpless
　　to keep her from what she must know.

　　[*The peasant women follow after* ETAIN. ANGUS, OWAIN *and* CONOR *enter, in the
　　midst of a heated conversation.* ANGUS *with his cane, limping still, but, like* OWAIN,
　　carrying bow and arrows. They are hunting.]

CONOR: A coward! Father . . . surely not!
　　Because I refuse to shoot at the wild birds?

OWAIN: Because you refuse the challenge I make.

CONOR: I will not bring down a bird
　　when I have no need of feather or food.

OWAIN: What is it you fear, lad—that
　　I can shoot farther than you?

CONOR: If it's my strength you would test
　　I'll wrestle you in the yard
　　in front of the house, with all of your
　　people gathered to watch.

OWAIN: The one who offers the challenge sets the task.
　　Why do you cower from what I ask?

CONOR: I haven't the heart to spoil this dawn

[175]

with the hiss of an arrow and shriek
of a creature in pain. I'm barely awake
from a wonderful dream.

ANGUS: Did you spend the night dreaming in bed
or did you stray up the hills
to dance 'round the Beltane flames
till you woke too weakened to hunt?

CONOR: That's it, of course. The old song, sung at the Beltane feast. I heard
it once as a boy, sung by a girl named Etain. But last night it seemed to
be sung in my dreams. The song and a vision of free flying birds. I
cannot kill what I dreamed.

ANGUS: Pah . . . it's four years since I wasted my time on that rite whose force
and power are gone.

OWAIN: It's an empty form. I feel the reason is gone.

ANGUS: Aye, it's become a womanish thing: silly steps and shrill voices—
womanly concerns. There's no woman at all can conceive a ritual dance
equal in force to a man's. But I thought you preferred womanish
things. . .

OWAIN: What do you mean?

ANGUS: Well, Lord, look at your son lying there on the ground, ensnared
by a womanish song.

OWAIN: Get up, boy, get up. There's no time to mope on the hunt.

CONOR: "Bless me and all living things I love," I can't get those words out of
my head.

OWAIN: Hush! I'll have a shot at that bird.

[*They fall silent.* OWAIN *takes aim and shoots an arrow into the air.*]

ANGUS: Wounded, but not brought down. Let me finish the task.

[ANGUS *aims and shoots. We hear the twang of the bow, the arrow whistling through
the air and the shriek of the creature in pain. We also hear* CONOR *crying out with the*

bird, as if he's been wounded, too.]

Pierced her clear through.

OWAIN: Well done. It's fallen there by the rocks. What's wrong with you, son? You bother me with your sounds.

CONOR: Father, call off the hunt. I seem to be one with those birds.

ANGUS: Ho . . . there's a fine bird in full flight.

[*He takes aim and shoots. Again, we hear the sounds of the bow and the arrow, and the shriek of the bird. Conor cries out with the bird.*]

OWAIN: Conor, be still.

ANGUS: A hit! Lord, forgive me for firing first. 'Twas a moment had to be seized. Is your son all right, Lord?

OWAIN: He's fine. Stand up, Conor, stand up.

CONOR: Father, stop the hunt. I am one with those birds.

OWAIN: Stop whining at me, boy. Act your age.

ANGUS: Don't blame your son. It was you, after all, who forbade the rite that might make him a man . . . in which you, Lord, would slaughter the puck and take for yourself the strength in the puck goat's blood. Had he been raised on that rite, he wouldn't be cowering now at the hunt.

OWAIN: Quiet, a shot.

[*Again we hear the arrow and bow, but not the scream of the bird, and* CONOR *is still.*]

ANGUS: Too bad. Have you thought to bring the rite back? There's of course some who say such dances and play have no magic power at all, but I'm not inclined to agree. Look at the way the flames of Beltane have sapped the strength of your son. Ah, there's a beautiful bird. Will you try your luck, Lord? [*Arrow and bow sounds.*] A miss . . . oh, well . . . Its flight is a thing to behold. Glorious, bold. Of course, ritual acts have no power in and of themselves . . . yet an idea that's given clear shape the

[177]

people are likely to accept. Since you forbade the fight with the puck the people are left with the womanish ways of Beltane or the womanish ways of the monk. Quick Lord, a shot! [*But* OWAIN *is lost in thought.*] Fled. My Lord, have you thought to revive that fight?

OWAIN: It has come to my mind.

ANGUS: Aye, those were glorious days. You ought to have seen us then, Conor, my lad. We were two glorious men. I shared with the king whatever I had. The rites I led and whatever I had in my bed. My daughter, eh, Lord, and the puck, both at the time you were needing new blood.

CONOR: You sicken me with your talk.

OWAIN: Quiet! A shot.

[*Again, bow, arrow, and shriek. Again,* CONOR *cries out.*]

ANGUS: Wounded, but flown out of sight. What's wrong with you, lad? Those women up in the hills have sapped the strength of your son, my Lord, and your aim is not what it was. You're not likely again to have one woman swelled full with child and another slim one in your bed. And he, Lord, well, your line seems to be done. It's a womanly thing he's become. You ought to have brought that rite back long ago.

OWAIN: Conor, pick up your bow. You will bring down the next bird that flies overhead.

CONOR: I will not destroy a beauty I've loved.

OWAIN: You dishonor this land with your cowardly ways. You will bring down a bird or not think of yourself as my son.

CONOR: I will wrestle you in the yard. But I will not kill what I've loved.

ANGUS: It's a pity, truly it is. You killed what you loved at your birth. Ripped your mother apart, so Brigit the midwife has said. Now she comes haunting you in the shape of a bird. Isn't it so? It's the ones we've hurt most hold us most in their spell. Quick, pick up your bow.

[ANGUS *and* OWAIN *take aim and shoot. Arrow and bow and bird scream. But*

[178]

CONOR *is silent.*]

ANGUS: Two arrows right on the mark and that glorious free-flying creature is ours. And your son, Lord, is still. He did not cry out. Together, my Lord, we are strong. The king and the maker of masks. [*In confidence*] Look how we've released the lad from the fiendish spell he's been in.

OWAIN: Quick, lad, you've time for a shot. Slay that bird coming now into view. [*Conor is still.*] slay her, I say, or you'll lose the bed under my roof. [*Conor looks at his bow.*] Bring that bird down, Conor, now. Bring her down or I'll not call you my son.

CONOR [*suddenly angered beyond control*]:
    Right, father, right, if you wish.
    I'll slay that bird in the sky.
    Why not!

    [*He shoots. We hear the bird's cry.*]

    There's a beauty I dreamed that is dead.
    And another one flown into view. Watch.

    [*He shoots again. We hear the shriek of the bird as it falls.*]

    My aim is better than yours.
    I can slay whatever I choose.

    [*He turns the drawn bow and arrow towards his father.*]

OWAIN: Watch yourself, lad.

CONOR: It's only a joke. [*He laughs.*]
    I'm your son, after all, am I not?
    We are three glorious men on the hunt.
    I'll go claim the corpses I've killed.
    Three hunters should share their spoils.
    There's only one thing you have that I don't.
    It's a pity Etain is gone.
    She's the one I should conquer and tame.
    Your daughter, old man? She's wounded, but not brought down.
    Lord Conor can finish the task you each tried and failed.

    [OWAIN *moves to strike him across the face.* CONOR *steps back.*]

[179]

CONOR: It's only a joke.
    I'll go claim the corpses I killed for your praise.

[*Exiting,* CONOR *nearly collides with* IAN, *who comes limping, holding an arrow in his hand.*]

ANGUS: The boy oversteps himself.

OWAIN: Silence! I will revive that fight with the puck.

IAN: Look, I've been struck.
    Oh, its quite all right.
    The arrow was spent;
    I happened to be sitting under that bird,
    caught up in a glorious dream-like sight.

OWAIN: Where are you hurt, man?

IAN: Here, in the thigh . . . it's a scratch, that's all that it is . . .
    well worth it, too, after the vision I had.

OWAIN: What were you dreaming about that kept you from moving out of
    the way?

IAN: Not dreaming, Lord, staring with my own eyes.
    A flight of wild crows flew over my head,
    a beautiful goddess ensnared in their web.
    O 'twas a wondrous sight, reminded me fierce
    of a wondrous love I once knew.

OWAIN: You're a fool, man, you always have been.
    You paid once for your bragging tongue.
    If I hear you giving voice to your silly
    visions and dreams, I'll slice your tongue
    out of your mouth. Now, go back to your flock!

[*To* ANGUS]

We will have the old ritual back.

ANGUS: As soon, Lord, as I have repaired the mask.
    The puck goat will die for the strength of the king,
    the wealth of the land, the yield of his line.

SCENE FOURTEEN

[CONOR *enters. He finds* ELEN *alone. His hands are dripping with blood. He is half mad after what he's done.*]

CONOR: Look, Elen, look.
　　For the love of my father and yours
　　I baptized myself in their faith.
　　Do you think I am saved from their wrath?

ELEN [*for a moment thinking he has perhaps killed them*]:
　　I will call Brother Vincent from prayer.

CONOR: I have no need of the monk.
　　I am one with the men on the hunt.
　　I beat them fair at their sport.
　　Now I'll have the spoils of their game. First, I'll take you.
　　When I'm done, I'll hunt out the girl named Etain.
　　They've aged you for me. You're like strong liquor.
　　When I've drunk I'll go taste the sweet-smelling girl.
　　I'll take her like I took those birds.
　　I'll come back with Etain trailing behind.
　　But I work the tale in reverse. I'll taste of you, first.

ELEN: Stay where you are. You have nothing to do with me.

CONOR: Wrong, Elen, wrong.
　　I've heard the tales that are told.
　　How you pleasured my father while my mother died.
　　How you pleasured my father and yours
　　while two women they wed lay alone in their graves.
　　Now the daughter will pleasure the son.

ELEN: He is still hunting me.

CONOR: Wrong. You are mine.
　　I hunt in his stead.

[181]

Old and weak as he is, he has
given you over to me.
See: [*he holds up his hands*]
I stink with the blood of the kill.

[CONOR *approaches her.* ELEN *holds her ground. She is strangely calm. Suddenly she
feels pity for* CONOR, *for what he has been forced to become.*]

ELEN: Give me your hand.
[*She lifts up his bloody hand and runs it down her cheek, painting her face with the
blood. Now she lifts his other bloody hand and paints his face with it.*]

We have mated here in the sun.
I could not be more yours than I am.
The rage we have felt
marks us and makes us one.

[*They stand still for a moment, as if suspended in time.*]

The work of the carver's hand is finally done.
We two stuck in this pose.
You craving a woman to hold and I growing cold under your touch.
Conor, go from this place. Seek what you need.
I have found comfort in my God.

[ANGUS *and* IAN *enter.*]

ANGUS: Puffed up from the hunt as you were
I thought you had gone to conquer a goddess or two.
You're wasting your time on that one.

IAN: Aye, it's a quest we all share, Conor,
it's true. A goddess who beckons to us,
over the hill, out from the shore.
Today the same dream has earned me a wound
in the thigh and a threat on my life.

ANGUS: Sure. It's queens and goddesses you'll be seeking till you learn a
woman's a woman. Each one has something inhuman in her that
batters the heart like a wave and leaves a man weak on the shore.
You'll be seeking to conquer that inhuman thing; you'll fail as each of
us does.

CONOR: Shut your mouth, old man.

ANGUS: There's no cause for anger at me. I never betrayed you. But women will do it again and again. Go off on your quest, now, be gone. Go find the goddess who will forgive the lad who murdered his mother the day he was born.

CONOR: I should kill you for that.

ANGUS: Sure, if you could. You're weak, lad. Just like that cold one there. [*He points to Elen.*] The ones whose mothers were killed by a hard birth never outlive that death.

ELEN: Conor, don't listen to him. Come. I'll walk with you as far as the path.

ANGUS: Come back when you have a tale to tell. Then we can talk man to man.

CONOR: When I come back, you'd better be gone.

ELEN: Come away from him.

[CONOR *and* ELEN *exit.*]

IAN: Ah, I wish I was young again.
　　　Wasn't it grand chasing dreams,
　　　and catching one long enough
　　　to feel the warmth of her flesh
　　　and raise the wrath of a king?

ANGUS: Do you like the king's threats?

IAN: Do you think I'm dumb?
　　　I tremble with fear. I grow numb.
　　　Still, it is fun stirring him up.
　　　He's a fine silly man, caught in his web just like us
　　　though we don't own his land or share in his wealth.

ANGUS: Yet he shares in your dreams.

IAN: I suppose that's usual enough. Poor folk can better
　　　imagine delight, having none, than the rich who have lost

[183]

the power to dream. That's why we're around, I suppose,
to care for the land and the herds and do the heart's hard work.

ANGUS: And why are they here, do you think?

IAN: Why that's easy enough . . .
They're here to live off our work,
they're here to steal our dreams.
They're here to scare us with threats.
They're here to eat what we cook, kill what we raise,
tease and misuse us, punish and abuse us.
They're here to destroy our land,
trample us down, scorn us and hate us,
mock us and make us dance to their tune,
then pay them the tribute they ask for,
treating us as if we were fools.

ANGUS: Quiet. That's enough. While you were dreaming and being stuck, I
made the king vow to revive the fight with the puck.

IAN: Well, you'd better look for another goat, my friend. There's no way
I'll stick my neck in that mask again.

ANGUS: You'll play the puck but we'll alter the plot one small bit.
This time, the king will not live.
I've poisoned the sword you will use.
You and I will inherit the land, and his crown.

IAN: Angus, you jest.
I could do no such thing! Stab a king!

ANGUS: He did it to you, after all.
If you can pay him in kind, Elen will be your queen.

IAN: Me, a king with a queen!
Angus, what luck. Do I dare? I do not. Take your plot
somewhere else. I could not. Why not? After all, I know how.
It's the plot I've dreamed and redreamed many years.
Me, a king with a queen! Angus, you can be sure
I'll always be grateful to you. Have no fear.
You've won the ear of a king!

SCENE FIFTEEN

[*The yard in front of* OWAIN's *house. The women sit at their work of carding and spinning.* ETAIN *helps with the wool, but her eyes wander down to the shore where she sees a heron flying free by the sea.*]

ETAIN: Look at that beautiful bird,
   silver and blue and alive,
   sailing out over the wave
   till sky and sea seem to merge
   in the beat of the blue heron's flight.

[*She rises and runs like the bird.*]

   I wish I was that bird,
   stirring the wings of the heart
   out of its own delight.

[*She runs like the bird, then suddenly stops, shrieks in pain as if wounded and falls in a swoon to the ground.*]

FIOLA [*motioning to the others to stay seated*]:
   He's on his way up from the shore.

CLEEVNA: He's brought down the bird.

DIEDRE: Aye, pierced it clear through.

MEENA: It lies in a heap on the broken side of a rock.

FIOLA: Hush, here he comes.

[OWAIN *enters carrying bow and arrows. He sees* ETAIN *on the ground.*]

OWAIN [*half in jest*]: Who is this fallen asleep? [*He approaches her.*]
   Get up, child, get up.
   Do you need food?

Are you too weak for this work?

[*Slowly* ETAIN *rises to a sitting position. She tosses her head.*]

ETAIN: You shot the bird from the sky.
  Did you not know it was me,
  it was you? Do you not know
  what you do?

THE WOMEN: Hush, Etain, hush. She is young.
  Lord, forgive her her tongue.

OWAIN: What is your name?

ETAIN: Death, sorrow, grief.
  I am what's left of the bird
  you brought down for sport.

OWAIN [*seizing her arm, shaking her*]: Come to your senses.
  What is your name, girl, your name?

ETAIN: I am Etain,
  spirit of what you destroyed,
  spirit of what you have lost.

OWAIN [*silent for a moment*]: You have come hunting me with one's
  sorrow filled voice and the other's
  untamable eyes.

ETAIN [*standing*]: You didn't kill it for food.
  You shot it because it flew
  'twixt the sky and the sea
  till it seemed like a monster to you.

OWAIN: It had caught the light of the sun
  and the deep shadows of the wave.
  It was one with the sky and the sea.
  It seemed untouchable by me.

[ETAIN *drops her heavy cloak, revealing herself in the shimmering garment the women wear on the mountain. She rises slowly.*]

ETAIN: Why have you done this thing,
    breaking the world apart?

OWAIN: We either break ourselves or something else;
    that is the secret of life.
    Then we live with the death we have made
    or die from the death we denied.
    You are young yet and do not know.

ETAIN: You stepped on a shell
    as you spoke. Once again you have trampled
    the world underfoot. When will you learn
    we are creatures of life? Death is only the way we return.

OWAIN: Why do you mourn that bird
    or the cracked and brittle shell?
    I have set their spirits free
    of their forms.

ETAIN: They were not yours to destroy.

OWAIN: What is mine, then—what?
    This heart that has been shuttered for so long
    it has forgotten pain?

ETAIN: It is no more yours than the bird.
    Only what you love is yours,
    only what quickens and rises up when you come.
    Alive, the bird was yours. Twisted and beautiful
    so was the shell. Alive they asked nothing of you,
    nor did they withold themselves.
    Broken and dead they scream in your ears for revenge,
    turning you deaf and hard, till you trample still more
    on the life you denied.

OWAIN: Your words fall like a curse made on my kind
    in ages past.

ETAIN: I have spoken the truth.

OWAIN: I have no choice but remain as I am.
    Your curse casts me into this form.

[187]

ETAIN: All things are changeable.

OWAIN: I do not feel so.

ETAIN: Look at my face. It will wither and age.
    It will crack like the bark of an old oak.
    My flesh will return to the earth.
    The nearer I come to death and decay
    from which the world takes its form
    the more I know of change.

OWAIN: Why have you come?

ETAIN: I don't know.
    I fear I dreamt you in a dream.

OWAIN: Fear, Etain? Fear?

ETAIN: I want to bury the bird you killed
    here by the sea so the salt and the sand
    can fold its flesh back in their warmth.
    Some of the feathers I'll pluck from the corpse
    to wear in my hair. I'll give them new life with my life.

OWAIN: You adorn yourself with something I killed
    in a moment's envy and greed. Do you
    become that selfsame thing, begging for death again?

ETAIN: I will mourn this bird, here, by the sea.

OWAIN: You can squat all day at the shore
    while the sun grows hot, then cold,
    and the corpse grows bloated and big.
    What will you know of death?
    The miraculous stopping of breath,
    the moment flight fails, the wondrous fall,
    the flesh ripped apart on the rock,
    blood rushing out from the throat,
    wings lying broken and bent.
    You can mourn that corpse till it rots
    in the stink of the sun, in the foul moonlight.
    You know nothing at all of the instant life stopped.

Have you ever stood silent and watched the beast that you
hunted and sought fly from your sight while desire tears
at your heart? You would know what the hunter has felt.
The minute the bird is conquered and falls, desire is done,
longing ends. Death is peace to the hunter who hunts
wild, untamable things. [*He takes her arm.*]
Follow me up the hill to the cave beneath three polished stones
where those who have died lie mixed with the dirt.
You have come taunting me with the sound of the woman
who once bore your name, who lies beneath those three stones.
You have come taunting me with your pride.

[*They exit. The peasant women take on a crow-like aspect again.*]

CROWS: She is caught,
    caught in his spell.
    Drawn to him like some broken thing.
    Quick, quick, up the hill.
    Macha must know her daughter is stolen away,
    carried by him under the earth,
    carried by him toward death.

SCENE SIXTEEN

[*Upon the hill.* MACHA *and* BRIGIT. MACHA, *already half crazed, paces, carrying torches, dressed in a long black robe, her hair loose, looking very tall and wild.* BRIGIT *attends her.*]

MACHA: I woke to a cry
    as if my flesh had been cut.
    Etain cried in grief.
    Etain has been taken from me.
    She is gone.
    Where can she be?

BRIGIT: I, too, heard the sound in my heart.
    Where is the child?
    No wild beast, unseen cliff,

falling rock would dare steal Etain from us.

MACHA: No, no, by human will she is gone.
    Little bird who once flew in my cave,
    little fish who once swam in my sea,
    why have you fled?

[*The* CROWS *appear.*]

BRIGIT: Hush, Macha, hush.
    The wild crows know the truth.

[BRIGIT *approaches them. There is flapping of wings and whispering, cackling sounds.*]

She is at the house.

MACHA: The house?

BRIGIT: At the shore.

MACHA: Why? Why is she there?

BRIGIT: She is drawn by something unknown.

MACHA: No. No. Everything full and mysterious
    dwells with us here in the hills.

BRIGIT: She is called by a touch.

MACHA: The sound of a voice.

BRIGIT: Owain, himself.

MACHA: Owain has captured Etain.
    Call her home.

BRIGIT: She is caught.

MACHA: No, she is not.

BRIGIT: She is under his spell.

MACHA: Call her back!

BRIGIT: I cannot. His voice
    is all she can hear.

MACHA: How can that be? My heart,
    my flesh. She could not run off.
    She is carried away by a man who has
    dreamed me his slave.

BRIGIT: She must go where he leads.

MACHA: He steals the treasure I made.
    He who has nothing to claim, claims my flesh
    as his own. He breaks Etain's will, carries
    her far from her self.

BRIGIT: Macha, do not grieve so.
    She will come back when she can.
    The daughter returns in the end,
    comes back from a longing in her heart
    to be where love starts.

MACHA: What do you know of such things?
    Childless and old, what do you know of my loss?

BRIGIT: I am yours to be used in your grief
    as you will; that is all I know.

MACHA: Bring her back.

BRIGIT: I am helpless to counter his spell.

MACHA: She is the woman he killed
    reborn to be slaughtered again.
    She is the one who beat him once,
    beaten down, now, by his force.

BRIGIT: She will not fall under his strength.
    She will meet death and laugh.

MACHA: She is a child in his grasp.

He is stronger than she.

BRIGIT: In body, perhaps.

MACHA: She is taken by him.
She is raped.
I am conquered at last.

Better the earth should perish and rot.
Better the earth should tremble and die
than Etain be stolen away. Better all life
should end than a child I birthed be abused,
a child I made be raped, be lost to herself.

You may be helpless, crone, but I am not.
Off and away foul-smelling birds,
bear Macha's anger down to the house.
Gnaw out the heart of him who has stolen my love.
Eat the seeds from the earth, kill the crops.
Pick out the eyes of the new-born lambs. Hide the sun.
Cause a quake in the earth until Etain is returned.

I will turn the world upside down under his feet.
Wipe out the crops, kill the sheep,
blight the house and the land
that have stolen my love.
Better the world be laid waste
than this sorrow allowed.

[MACHA *begins to pace, rending her garments, keening a wild keen.* BRIGIT *follows with the torchlights as the sky grows dark.*]

SCENE SEVENTEEN

[*Darkness.* OWAIN *and* ETAIN *approach the dolmen.* MACHA *paces in grief on the mountain top.*]

OWAIN: Here is the place.
Here, beneath these stones the path leads

toward the center of the earth, the common grave.

ETAIN: The birds are circling round the sun.
    They keep the light away.
    My mother grieves at losing me.
    I would return to her.

OWAIN: Go, then, if you will.
    I leave you free.

    [*She does not move.*]

    Or follow me into this sacred cave
    and learn the secret she would keep from you.

ETAIN: The birds are circling round the sun.
    They will destroy the crops
    and blight the land you have forgot
    in this mad search for death.
    Let me go back to her.

OWAIN: What are you afraid of, what?
    That one who gave you life
    will turn on you because you dare
    to touch the death
    in one whose name you bear?

ETAIN: I am free to follow where I will.
    I am not bound by her, nor you.

OWAIN: Then come.
    Within this cave you will learn
    all that made me slay the wild bird.

ETAIN: Death is not yours to tame.
    It is not man's.
    You cannot hunt death down.

OWAIN: What are you afraid of, what?
    That if you follow where I lead
    you will find out why you plucked the feathers
    from a corpse to braid into your hair?

ETAIN: The birds are circling round the sun.
    They will eat the crops and kill the lambs.
    The earth will take revenge if you forget
    death is ruled by life.
    I will return to her.

OWAIN: What are you afraid of, what?
    In her anger that you've gone
    she casts death upon the land?
    In her rage she will reveal to you
    the thrill she feels at killing
    what she birthed?
    Follow me into this cave.

[*The* CROWS *pick up the black ground-cloth, making the earth quake as* OWAIN *leads* ETAIN *into the cave beneath the dolmen. Overhead,* MACHA *emits a cry.*]

ETAIN: The earth convulses as we enter here.
    Let me return. The quake will end.

OWAIN: We must go deeper down.

ETAIN: The earth heaves up again.

OWAIN: She threatens us, but we will learn
    all she forbids. We must go deeper down.

ETAIN: The sky is dark.
    The earth breaks herself apart.
    I must go back.

OWAIN: Not before you understand the reason why
    the wild bird is slain.

ETAIN: Why do you drag me with you, why?
    All is dark and fearsome here.

OWAIN: Yes, you must see her as she is.
    You must see why men must fight and must destroy.
    We must go deeper down.

ETAIN: Stop. The earth convulses underneath my feet.

She heaves up dead, decaying things.
The stink of rotting flesh confuses all that lives.

OWAIN: Now you have come close,
    You smell, you sense, you see.
    We are nothing but this dirt, this dust.
    Here, Etain, are bones. [*He kicks them with his feet.*]
    Etain's bones lie underneath your feet.
    Touch. Smell. This is Etain:
    this stink, this rotted flesh.
    This is the life you love,
    for which you have been named.

ETAIN: You brought me to her grave.

OWAIN: Yes, I brought you here, to death,
    to death which eats us up, food for a vengeful appetite,
    and there is no escape. She takes the best of us before our time;
    leaves the worst for last. But all end here, a stink of bone
        and rotted flesh.
    And no one equals death, unless we kill the wild bird. In the moment
    that the blade goes through the throat, in the scream the victim makes,
    the killer commands death. The hunter
    does not wait. He spares no one. He bests death
    at death's game. He proves his strength and wins.

ETAIN: Now I know. I have come for this.
    Let me touch what you have touched.
    Let me feel with my hands those bones you kicked.

[ETAIN *takes up the bones. She caresses them. She holds them in her lap. She touches the earth with her hands. She paints her cheeks with dirt, the dirt made of* ETAIN's *rotted flesh.*]

Here are her bones, and here her flesh.
Dear, dear Etain. It was not death, but fear
that claimed you for her own. Yet what have I
to fear if this is what you have become?
You are the earth from which I grow.
I am Etain. One who loved you bore me
from herself, dragged me from the flesh
between her thighs, spat me out upon the ground.
What wild cry escaped her lips when you turned stiff

[195]

and died? What endless keen still echoes on the wind?
Yet she was bound to life. Mimicking the earth
that writhed beneath your corpse, what wild cry
escaped her lips when I was born? She was racked
by life. Mixed in the blood and filth
that flowed from her, I hid. Amid her grunts
and groans I called my name, Etain.
Looking down she dared respond: dared name me
for the dead, dared offer me her breast, dared love.
Though as I sucked she knew my head would break upon
the rock there at her feet; the sea would take me back;
or she could leave me for the birds to peck apart.
Each time I sucked she felt death's claim on her.
"Death is the mother who calls us back," "Death
is the lover we seek," she thought and rocked me
in her arms. "Life is the trembling babe who would
willingly shatter and break if I flung her down on these rocks."
"Life is all we might lose, all that we might not keep."
"Life is what comes from grief."
Till the light flows into this cave, I will lie here
cradling these bones. The wild bird is safe in my lap.

[*During this speech,* OWAIN *paints his own face with the dirt and
dust of* ETAIN. *Then he moves toward* ETAIN's *lap. She takes him into
her lap, and they sit; she holds him in her lap. Rocked there, he weeps.*]

SCENE EIGHTEEN

[*An eerie dark.* IAN *talks to the puck goat head.*]

IAN: It's you and me, again, chum.
The sky is as dark as it was,
the sun has been stolen away,
by what evil force do you think?
And we have been chosen to bring it back!
You look the same.
Age has not altered your charm.
But what about me, do I look like a king?

What do you think of the profile, the stance—
am I kingly enough, ugly mask? Wipe that smirk
off your face! [*He picks up the sword and flourishes it.*]
Am I kingly now? Answer me, brute, or I'll slice your tongue
out of your mouth!
You know a king when you hear a king speak.
You tremble and quake.
I'm ruthless and strong,
king of the land!

[CONOR *enters.*]

CONOR: King of the land?

IAN: Halt! What do you want!
   You've stepped on my land unannounced.
   My rival's son, halt and disarm.

CONOR: What are you ranting about?

IAN: You threaten me with your breath!
   I'll end that by cutting your throat!

[CONOR *grabs* IAN *by the throat.*]

CONOR: Say farewell to your silly talk!

IAN: Please, Lord, mercy, mercy, I beg.
   I was out of my mind, over my head.

   [CONOR *pushes him toward the ground, then lets him drop on his behind.*]

   Whew! Lord, you are good! Merciful. Brave.
   Just to your folk. Strong.

CONOR: Are all of my father's folk foolish as you?

IAN: Foolish? Of course. It's a foolish man we now serve.
   Lord, have you ever wanted to rule?
   Ask yourself that. . . . Of course, how could you not?
   Lord, you take the mask and this sword.
   Your father awaits a fight with the puck.
   You can challenge the man in full view.

[197]

You're young. You will win! You'll take the rule of the land.
You will bring back the warmth of the sun.
Lord, I'll always be loyal to you!

CONOR: I'm on my way somewhere else.
I'll challenge my father when I'm back.

[BRIGIT *enters.*]

BRIGIT: You were coming to us in the hills.

CONOR: Yes.

BRIGIT: For Etain.

CONOR: Yes.

BRIGIT: What do you want with the girl?

CONOR: She is mine.

BRIGIT: Yours?

CONOR: Yes. Mine. The one I dream of.

BRIGIT: She has fled.

CONOR: Tell me where she has gone.

BRIGIT: Her flight brings the dark on the land.

CONOR: I will bring her home.
I'll go where she hides.
I'll come back with Etain on my arm.
Then I'll get rid of my father.

IAN: Lord, that's a grand dream.

BRIGIT: In any case, dreamt too late.
Etain is with Owain, now.

CONOR: That's not so.

BRIGIT: She goes where he leads.

CONOR: He takes everything precious from me!
His greed blights the land.
He steals Etain.
Where are they? Where have they gone?

BRIGIT: They have disappeared.

CONOR: I'll kill him for this.

IAN: Excuse me, Lord, I happen to know, Lord Owain will be back to fight the puck goat in an hour or so. Here, let me lend you this mask. It's all right, really it is. Take my place.

CONOR: What would I want with your mask? I'll go as I am. I'll show him the man I've become. I'll take Etain back. She's mine.

BRIGIT: Your talk no longer suits you to her.

IAN: Lord, go disguised. Catch him off guard. If you go as you are, the people will interfere. But if the puck wins the people will see Owain is unfit to rule. Here, Lord, the mask and the sword.

BRIGIT: Give me the sword. [*She takes it and smells it.*] Poisoned. Angus did this. [*She spits on the sword and wipes it on her skirt.*] Poisoned the sword, just as he poisoned the faith. [*To* IAN] And you are part of the plot.

IAN: Poisoned! My Lord! I had no idea. No thought. He never told me that!

BRIGIT: Silence.

CONOR: I'll challenge him, yes. Fairly, I shall win the fight. There is no other way to set things right.

BRIGIT: Perhaps not.

CONOR: I'll wound him, that's all. Wound him in front of his folk. He'll be disgraced.

BRIGIT: Perhaps. But you'll be no better for that.

CONOR: He'll fear me, at last. I'll have the woman I want.

BRIGIT: Etain is not part of your fight.

CONOR: She will decide about that.

BRIGIT: You ought to decide something first. Is need for your father's love driving you?

CONOR: His love! Give me the sword. Brigit, bless me now.

BRIGIT: Go well, lad. Be open to all you don't know. Find all you must have.

IAN [to CONOR]: Lord, be brutal and strong. Challenge the king. Bring him down! [IAN puts the mask on CONOR.] You're the fertile puck from the mountain tops, fearless and wild. Bellow and kick. You will conquer the king!

[CONOR exits.]

Aye, it is a magical mask. But I had a narrow escape. I'm happy to give up the crown, if I don't have to risk my neck. Thanks, Brigit, thanks. I've had enough of Angus and his plots. But I can't resist watching this show. I'm off to see if Lord Owain eats dirt or kills his own child. Brigit, what a fine plot we have hatched. We're smarter than Angus, it seems; perhaps you and I . . .

BRIGIT: Will you silence your tongue!
This plot was made long ago
at the end of a fight Owain lost.
And we must hope the curse Macha
cast him in holds strong.

SCENE NINETEEN

[Dark. Sounds of the CROWS; ELEN and VINCENT talking in the yard.]

ELEN: The birds have picked the fields clean. They terrorize the new-born lambs. The people fear some ancient spirit's rage.

VINCENT: And you, my child?

ELEN: I wonder why such destruction is allowed. What does it signify?

VINCENT: What does it matter, child, if you have faith in God? What does it matter if the world should end as we stand wondering why? Our Lord redeems with everlasting life what nature scorns with scourges, plagues and death.

ELEN: The people fear starvation. They fear death. I cannot help but share the sorrows of those who work this land. I understand why they would call upon my father to prepare a rite that might ensure the sun's return.

VINCENT: When I went out of my father's house, I knelt before him in the dust. With a single gesture I tore off my clothes. I wanted nothing of the pagan world from which I'd come, nothing of his land, his wealth, nothing of the magic rites his superstition tied him to. In my hand I clutched one loaf of bread. But as I knelt there in the dust, a voice spoke in my ear. "Where is thy faith? In grain?" I dropped the bread upon the earth and stood. Naked I left my father's house, clothed in my heavenly father's love. This is what it means, my child, to renounce the old ways. You must cleave to nothing, no one, but your God. Where is your faith? In a pagan rite?

ELEN: No.

VINCENT: Then give up these earthly ties.

[ETAIN and OWAIN enter.]

OWAIN: Etain, never have I mourned my own wife's loss
until this night we spent within her grave.

ETAIN: Aye, you lay in my arms and wept the whole night through.

OWAIN: Etain, I am full of longing for my son.
If I wept for the losses of these years, I
rose wanting to see the child who has grown
from a babe to a man nurtured on nothing but
the stone I had made of my heart.
Vincent, have you seen my son?

ELEN: Conor has fled.

ETAIN: He will come back.
    We are each of us pulled to that source.
    Each must find out what called us to life.

[*Now the procession enters the yard. It is composed of* ANGUS *and the* PEASANT
WOMEN, *the* CHILDREN *from Act II and, also,* BRIGIT, *here to watch over the scene but
not to take part in it. The procession is full of need. It is an invocation and recalls the fear
of the people way back when this tale began.*]

PEOPLE [*singing*]: Each spirit of life bless our calling,
    each daimon who lives in each ridge,
    each spirit of plain and of field.
    Bless the need that we have for the sun to return.
    Bless the need that we have for the sun to return.

ANGUS: Here, lord, is a magical sword.
    You will slay the puck goat;
    then the land will revive, washed
    in the balm of that blood.

OWAIN: You're certain that is the plot?

ANGUS: Of course.

OWAIN: I read deception in your eyes.

ANGUS: You are nervous, my lord.
    Have I ever deceived you before?

OWAIN: The sword you gave to the puck,
    is it free of all poison or taint?

ANGUS: Lord, how can you ask such a thing?

OWAIN: I have lost trust in you.
    [*He takes the sword.*]
    Where is the puck?

ANGUS: In a moment, my lord, he will come.
    Till then, my lord, dance with the lady at your side,

[202]

and I will dance with my daughter. Come, Elen,
in the midst of this fearful dark,
let us recall what is finished and done,
a longing as harsh as the sun.

[*She turns away.*]

Can you not even look at me, girl?

ELEN: My eyes are turned inward
and all my desire has fled,
upward, toward my God.

[ELEN *drops down to her knees to pray with* VINCENT. OWAIN *and* ETAIN *join the head of the procession, which sings.*]

PEOPLE: Each spirit of life bless our calling,
each daimon who lives in each ridge.
Turn the birds from the evil they do.
Let the plague that we suffer be lifted.
Bless the need that we have for the sun to return.
Bless the need that we have for the sun to return.

[CONOR *appears, disguised as the* PUCK GOAT.]

The puck, the puck.
Let Lord Owain slay the puck.

[CONOR *approaches* OWAIN *and* ETAIN. *They separate from the procession.*]

OWAIN: What! Puck goat, have you come again!
Image from another time.

PUCK: We will fight to return the sun to the land.

OWAIN: Yes, we will spill your blood on the earth.

PUCK: Or yours. Let go of the woman you hold.

OWAIN: My business with this woman is my own.

PUCK: I will not let you sully her with age.

OWAIN: She is untouched and stays untouched with me.

[203]

PUCK: She's mine. I'll have her once I've beaten you.

OWAIN [*laughs*]: So. The prince has come—
    half goat, half man—to claim the maiden for his own.

PUCK: Yes. Once I've spilled your blood,
    I'll pour life into her.

OWAIN: You speak too soon.

ETAIN [*moving away*]: You will not barter me between yourselves.
    Those who survive are victors each
    and find me where they seek eternal things.

    [*She goes.*]

OWAIN: Go, catch her, goat,
    if you claim her as your own.

PUCK: Don't call me by that name.

OWAIN: Why not? You are the image of a puck,
    yet seem to lack ability to mount.
    Do you wear a mask to masquerade at all
    you cannot do?

PUCK: The king's cloak you wear . . .
    does it hide your feebleness from view?
    Raise up your sword. I will conquer one
    whose rule brings a curse upon the land.

    [OWAIN *draws his sword and* CONOR *draws his.*]

OWAIN: I will strike first, if you do not;
    my blood is hot. You've thrown a challenge
    at me before my folk.
    Come, goat, do you fear this fight?

    [*Slowly, they begin to circle one another.*]

PUCK: I hate the man who calls me by that name.
    I am not an image to be scorned.

OWAIN: You are a mocking shape I would destroy.

CONOR: And you an empty shell called king.

OWAIN: You seek my power from me.

PUCK: What belongs to me, I claim.

OWAIN: You cannot have my strength.

PUCK: Your strength will die with you.

OWAIN: Goat. You are not fit to rule.

PUCK: As fit as one who taunts with cruelty.

OWAIN: The power of a king rises upward, from the earth.

PUCK: It does. I will receive it from your dust.

OWAIN: No, goat. I will drink your blood.

PUCK: My blood will not empower you.
    The goat will slay the king.

OWAIN: You have been bewitched to do this deed
    by one who seeks my death.

PUCK: I stand here on my own.
    It is our fight. No one has interfered.

OWAIN: Then, remove your mask.
    Or is that ugly face your own?

PUCK: You will see me as I am,
    and you will still be blind.

[CONOR *removes the mask, handing it to* ANGUS, *who is shocked.*]

OWAIN: Conor, my son.
    Put down your sword.
    There will be no blood.

CONOR: No. Who better for me to destroy than you
who never looked upon my face
with any but a cold, hardend look.

OWAIN: All that I did not have to give
reproached me from your eyes.
I was compelled to turn away.

CONOR: And I compelled to trail you like a dog,
searching your angry ways for who I was.

OWAIN: I was alone.

CONOR: I was begging you to see:
out of all you lost
you had been given me.

OWAIN: I saw my faults manifest in you;
I saw nothing else.

CONOR: I need not have removed the mask.
I am still the wild puck goat.
We challenged one another from the start.

OWAIN: It is a challenge I have just begun to meet.

CONOR: Too late. We will have this fight.

OWAIN: No, the fight is at an end.
Put down your sword, my son.

[OWAIN *lowers his sword, but keeps it in his hand.*]

CONOR: You can't disarm me with a softened word.

OWAIN: You are my child, I will speak gentleness to you.

CONOR: Too late. Beneath this sword you will grow childlike.

[*He lunges at his father.* OWAIN *steps away and is wounded, perhaps in the thigh.*]

ANGUS: A king who lets another strike the opening blow cannot rule the
land. The crops would die beneath a coward king.

OWAIN: The king is less a coward than he's ever been.

CONOR: Pick up your sword.
    You go first. The carver's next.

ANGUS: A son who turns against his father for no cause cannot rule the
    land.

OWAIN: Wrong. His is the only cause to whose wisdom I submit.
    [OWAIN *throws down his sword.* ANGUS *reaches for it.* OWAIN *steps on it.*]
    Go. We will be left alone.

VINCENT: Denounce that pagan criminal who reaches for your sword.

OWAIN: What he does denounces him.
    The next turn on the lethal wheel of time, Vincent, is yours.

VINCENT: I will build a church upon this land.

OWAIN: You will. I lend my strength to something still unlived.

CONOR: Yes, kill me if you can.

OWAIN: I would kill your rage. Then, the man you are can live.

ANGUS [*to* CONOR]: Beat him while you can. He's always hated you.

OWAIN: No, son. I loved you with a love that had no form.

ANGUS: Are you too weak to do the job?

    [*He reaches for* CONOR's *sword.*]

CONOR [*threatening* ANGUS, *who backs off*]:
    Leave us alone. Your plot is finished, done.

OWAIN: My son is the strongest man I've ever known. He has fought
    his whole life through to make me see him as he is.
    Vincent, look, I follow your example in all ways.
    I, too, abandon all that I have been.
    I give up the robe, the vest, the sword, these jewelled weights,
    the boots that trod the land where others worked,

this cloth, woven by another's hand. I kneel naked in the dust
before my son. My son, who rouses feelings I have feared
far more than I have feared the battle I disown. Go, leave us alone.

[*The* PEOPLE *exit.*]

Can I disarm you, now, my child?

[OWAIN *reaches up and pulls* CONOR *down to him.* CONOR *sits, and rocked in his
father's arms, he covers both their bodies with his cloak.*]

OWAIN: Until I took you in my arms I thought
    there was not comfort in the world enough to fill my empty heart.
    I had changed desire into death, until I rocked you back and forth.

CONOR: Father, I dreamed this touch and thought
    it was my mother who I sought.
    I felt I would remain a bent and broken thing,
    seeking after what is dead.

[*The two rock slowly back and forth. They come into direct relationship with one
another. They grow intimate, as the arc of their movement rises from effort into joy.
Their motion is sensual, erotic, life-renewing. At its peak,* CONOR *speaks.*]

CONOR: Father, you have brought me whole into the world.

OWAIN: Now, at last, I know your body as my own.
    Flesh of my flesh, my son.

[*We hear the sound of the* CROWS.]

CONOR: There, upon the hills, I see three shadows
    in the evening light. Two run towards each other and embrace.
    The other, bent and slow, stands quiet and apart.
    Do you see the shadows I describe? Did you feel the wind
    blow as they ran? Can you sense the stillness come as they draw close?

OWAIN: Yes, I see them there. Brigit, Macha and Etain—
    three who worked the mystery of birth
    and caught us in the spell they've woven for all time.

CONOR: Come, father, let us go. We, too, were made
    to live free on the hills, borrowing from nature

what we need. Let us begin our climb.

[*They rise and as they go, we see the women running towards each other, and the* CROWS *joining them.*]

ETAIN: Mother! Mother!

CROWS: She is home.

ETAIN: Mother, I'm back!

MACHA: Precious child!

CROWS: She is grown.

MACHA: Grown, the wild crows sang.

CROWS: Grown! Macha saw. It was true.

ETAIN: I am strong.

CROWS: Strong, Macha's heart sang.

MACHA: You are beautiful, bold.

CROWS: Etain's eyes shone.

MACHA: A woman full grown.

ETAIN: Yes, mother, yes.

CROWS: Macha smiled.

MACHA: A woman full grown, in full strength.

ETAIN: Mother, it's true.

CROWS: I am proud, Macha's look said.

MACHA: You are wise.

CROWS: As wise as Macha, perhaps, the girl's heart jumped.

ETAIN: Brigit, I'm back.

BRIGIT So I see.
   The child comes back in the end.
   Comes back from a longing in her heart
   to be where love starts.

ETAIN: Mother, sing me a song.
   I have been far away.
   Welcome me back. I am grown.

MACHA: I will sing you a song from another time.

[*She sings and the* CROWS *join her.*]

There is no love like the love that I bear for Etain.
I bore her out of myself. All that I am, she is.
I am the sea, Etain the wave. I am the ground,
she is the hill; I am the sky, she is the sun, the moon.
All that has form she is. I am all that is formless,
senseless, wild, all that is feared or desired.
She is the hill, the wave, the light.
She is the mark of my strength.
She is the proof of my love.

[CONOR *and* OWAIN *appear. They are welcomed by a gesture or a look. Silence. The sun sets.*]